# REALLY LIVING 2

Other books by Don Schneider
with Ken Wade

*Really Living*

DON SCHNEIDER with KEN WADE

*More*
stories
of lives
changed
by Jesus

# REALLY LIVING 2

Pacific Press® Publishing Association
Nampa, Idaho
Oshawa, Ontario, Canada
www.pacificpress.com

Cover design by Gerald Lee Monks
Cover design resources from The Adventist Media Center
Inside design by Aaron Troia

The authors assume full responsibility for the accuracy of all facts and quotations as cited in this book.

You can obtain additional copies of this book by calling toll-free 1-800-765-6955 or by visiting http://www.adventistbookcenter.com.

Scripture quotations marked ESV are from The Holy Bible, English Standard Version® (ESV®), copyright © 2001 by Crossway, a publishing ministry of Good News Publishers. Used by permission. All rights reserved.

Scriptures quoted from KJV are from the King James Version.

Scriptures quoted from NKJV are from The New King James Version, copyright © 1979, 1980, 1982, Thomas Nelson, Inc., Publishers.

Scripture quotations marked NIV are from the HOLY BIBLE, NEW INTERNATIONAL VERSION®. Copyright © 1973, 1978, 1984 by International Bible Society. Used by permission of Zondervan Publishing House. All rights reserved.

Scripture texts credited to NRSV are from the New Revised Standard Version of the Bible, copyright © 1989 by the Division of Christian Education of the National Council of the Churches of Christ in the USA. Used by permission. All rights reserved.

Library of Congress Cataloging-in-Publication Data:

Schneider, Don C., 1942-
  Really living 2 : more stories of lives changed by Jesus / Don
Schneider with Ken Wade.
     p. cm.
  ISBN 13: 978-0-8163-2449-1 (pbk.)
  ISBN 10: 0-8163-2449-2 (pbk.)
  1. Christian biography. I. Wade, Kenneth R., 1951- II. Title. III.
Title: Really living two.
  BR1700.3.S36 2011
  277.3'0830922—dc22
  [B]
                                                            2010045116

11 12 13 14 15 • 5 4 3 2 1

# Contents

# Care for Your Enemies

## Nikolaus Satelmajer

"You better stop, or they'll start shooting at us!" Nikolaus Satelmajer yelled at the man in the driver's seat beside him. Ahead on a dark rural road in the country of Nik's birth, two soldiers with automatic weapons stood menacingly beside the road. To Nik it looked like an official checkpoint of the type one didn't dare ignore.

It was a time of war, and the two pastors were traveling on back roads because the main highways had all been bombed into oblivion.

The reason they were traveling at night, Nik told me, was that it is easier to see tracer bullets in the dark and know when somebody is shooting at you.

The driver cramped on the brakes, and they screeched to a stop just in time. But as they looked around, they realized that they weren't at a checkpoint after all. These two soldiers were out there on their own—probably AWOL—and definitely drunk. And they wanted a ride.

"What did you do?" I asked.

"We didn't have any choice. We gave them a ride."

Once the men were in the car, Nik realized the situation

was even more dangerous than he had first thought, because the soldiers were from a different region of the former country of Yugoslavia than he was. If he dared say a word, his speech would give him away, and they would take him for an enemy. The fact that his family had left that part of the world many years before and that he now carried an American passport would make little impression on their sodden minds.

This frightening episode was just one of many tense moments Nik experienced while making seven trips to the strife-torn region of the world that had been known as Yugoslavia when he was born there just before the end of World War II.

Many things about Nik's story are amazing—not the least of which is that he claimed to never in his life have felt more at peace than he did while traveling in that war zone. But to me, the most amazing part of his story is that he was there in the first place, that he was willing to go back and risk his life bringing humanitarian aid to a country that had rejected his family, nearly starved them to death, and finally driven them out.

Nik's story begins near the end of World War II, but his family's history in Yugoslavia, in the part now known as Bosnia and Herzegovina, goes back even further.

During the 1700s, many German families moved eastward from their native land and settled in Russia, Romania, and other countries. For many generations, Nik's ancestors had lived in what came to be Yugoslavia after World War I. During World War II, there were nine families of Satelmajers all living and farming in the same area.

When the war ended with Germany's defeat, the Communist partisans who had been fighting against the Germans in Yugoslavia came to power, and within two days after the German surrender, Communist soldiers showed up at all of the

Satelmajer farms, telling Nik's family to get ready to move—they were being evicted from their land.

Not knowing what to expect, Nik's mother packed a suitcase and came out into the yard. One of the soldiers looked at her with a sneer, then drove his bayonet into the side of the suitcase, ripping it apart. Then the soldier dumped the clothes his mother had so carefully packed out in the barnyard and let the animals trample on them.

With nothing to their names except the clothes on their backs, the family was marched off to a makeshift concentration camp in a nearby city.

This was no real camp, Nik told me. "What they did, they just threw up a barbed-wire fence and threw the five thousand or so prisoners in there, and you just had to fend for yourself. There were some buildings, some barns, stuff like that, and the fortunate ones found a place in a barn. Otherwise you built lean-tos or whatever you had."

Nik was about eighteen months old when this happened, and soon he was fighting for his life. "The children used to get sick—dehydrated usually—the food was terrible. Usually they had bean soup that was more water than beans, and moldy corn bread. That was our staple. And even that was rationed."

Sanitation was almost nonexistent, and the children were the first to suffer. "What they used to do was take the children off on the side to die, and they would just wait until the child died. It was just a routine thing.

"So they took me there, because they looked at me, and they figured I was dying. My mother would be there with me—they would take turns. My father would be there, my aunts and uncles, my older cousins, just watching me."

Just watching him, wondering when he would die.

But then somebody else came into the picture.

"We had made friends with a Catholic priest," Nik told me. "He came over and said to my mother, 'I would like to pray for the boy.'

"He prayed for me, and she told him how I couldn't keep anything down—even water—nothing. So he said, 'Let me try something.'

"He went back to his little corner, and he had some uncooked coffee, and he brought that coffee and opened my mouth and put the ground-up coffee on my tongue, and it startled me, it shocked me. And for a few seconds, I stopped screaming and swallowed whatever was on my tongue."

The priest kept up this treatment, putting on a little more and a little more, until finally Nik was calm enough for his mother to try giving him a little water. The water stayed down this time, and Nik eventually recovered.

"That man saved your life," I said.

"He did, and I met him. In 1990 was the first time I ever went back there, after we were allowed to finally leave the country, and he was now a Catholic bishop in northern Bosnia."

When Nik asked the bishop if he remembered that story, the bishop replied, "So many terrible things happened—I don't remember that specific instance. But once in a while, even in the midst of horror, God gives us a chance to do something that is good."

Something good in the midst of horror is what Nik was trying to do the night they picked up the drunken soldiers. Because by the 1990s Yugoslavia had descended once again into turmoil, ethnic hatred, and killing.

In the 1940s, Nik's family lived in the concentration camp for about a year. He has been told that there were about five thousand people all together in the camp, and that of the children his age who were interned there, only seven survived.

He also heard that one of his aunts was held in a camp about two hundred miles away where, over the course of three years, ninety thousand people were killed or died from disease or starvation.

"My family was among the lucky ones," Nik says. "Some families were kept in the camp for three years."

While they were in the camp, the able-bodied family members were forced to work cleaning up the rubble left over from the war. Nik's father was a resourceful man, who would bring home bits of aluminum gleaned from the wreckage of airplanes that had been shot down. From the aluminum, he would make combs to give to guards as gifts, in hopes of gaining their friendship. Later he made small suitcases using the crudest of tools. He even had to make his own rivets. Nik still has one of those little aluminum suitcases today.

In that type of environment, family and friendships became very important. There would sometimes be several days in a row when even the moldy corn bread and watery soup wouldn't be delivered. At times like that, Nik's family members all pulled together. There were about sixty Satelmajers in the camp, and if any one of them was able to find a food source, the food would be shared with the whole family. By all working together, they managed to survive a day at a time.

"Were you Christians then?" I asked.

"We were. We were Sabbath keepers, and that made it very hard in the camp. My father had to face the camp commander, and the camp commander would say to him, 'You have a choice. Either you go to work, or we shoot you.' And my father said to him, 'What you do, sir, is your choice. What I do is my choice. I'm not going to work.'

"They kept threatening him week after week after week, but they didn't shoot him."

Religion played an important part in survival and in keeping the family together. When I asked Nik whether there were times when he began to wonder if there was a God who cared about all the suffering going on, he replied by telling me about his very spiritual, close-knit family.

"Even when they released us from the camp, life was really, really hard. We were no longer citizens of the country. We had lost our property. You know, I would wonder— what's this all about? But I found a certain warmth in the home that erased the horrors that I experienced from day to day.

"I remember Sabbaths in particular. Friday afternoon, in the midst of the most terrible circumstances, when my father later on had to go to labor camps and work for the government without any pay, and Friday afternoons we would be together with other family members, and invariably one of them would say, 'Thank God, the Sabbath is coming.' And that made it a sacred time. We had no church; we had to meet in secret in our home. But that didn't matter. The special sacredness of the Sabbath coming in the midst of the horrors—that has always stayed with me."

After Nik's family had been in the camp for about a year, a group of them were ordered to pack up to leave. The next day, they found themselves being marched deep into the forest. Word quickly spread among the prisoners of what usually happened to people who were marched into the woods—they were never heard from again.

"We felt that was the end," Nik said, "that we were going to be executed."

But the next morning, instead of being executed, they were released. "They just let us go. I mean, it was not like 'Here's a bus ticket,' or 'We'll take you home.' It was just 'You're on your own.'"

They made their way to their homes, which had been totally ransacked and destroyed and were totally unlivable.

But they had good neighbors—Muslim neighbors, in fact.

"We found out that Muslims, when they're your friends, they're really your friends," Nik told me. "They risked the anger of the government, and they took us into their homes. Even though we were declared enemies of the state."

While living with their neighbors, the Satelmajers were able to repair their homes, and after a few months, they moved back to their own farms. But because they were no longer considered citizens of Yugoslavia, they didn't own their farms anymore.

Having been declared enemies of the state and deprived of their citizenship, they had few privileges and many responsibilities. So they naturally began looking for ways to escape their predicament. West Germany had declared an open immigration policy for any German people living in Communist countries, but Yugoslavia would not let them leave.

Then word went around that the government would allow people to emigrate to the United States—all you had to do was register with the local government, and the information would be passed on to the U.S. consulate.

Nik's parents and several other relatives jumped at the chance.

But the offer turned out to be just a ploy to find out who was disloyal. Three of Nik's uncles were thrown in prison just for having registered their desire to leave the country. Nik's own parents were also arrested, but for some reason they were not sent to prison.

Finally, with the aid of an attorney, they found a legal way to leave the country. "But the final insult," Nik told me, "was to say that before you leave, you have to cancel your citizenship, and to do that you have to pay a fee. And it was a large fee—equivalent to one year's wage for just the three of us.

"My father said, 'But we're not citizens anymore. Here's the document that says you took our citizenship away.'"

The government official's response? " 'Oh, you've been made a citizen again,' and so that was the final insult," Nik said. They had to pay the fee.

Finally though, they managed to leave Yugoslavia. Nik has a precious memory of his first Christmas in freedom. They were living in Hamburg, Germany, and he remembers listening to Christmas music on the radio, and for the first time not being worried that this religious activity might be reported to officials who would consider it a crime.

### Serving his enemies

This story of persecution and hardship is all background to a phone call that came to Nik's home in Canada one morning in 1991. The way he told me the story, I couldn't help but think of the story of Paul's Macedonian call in the book of Acts. "A vision appeared to Paul in the night. A man of Macedonia stood and pleaded with him, saying, 'Come over to Macedonia and help us' " (Acts 16:9, NKJV).

If you look at a map, you'll notice that Croatia is not far from Macedonia.

Here's how Nik told the story of his Croatian-Macedonian call: "One morning, the phone rings. . . . I answer. A man says to me, 'Do you speak Croatian?' That's one of the languages in that part of the world. I said, 'Yes, I can manage.' I didn't know who the man was."

It turns out that the man on the other end was part of the Seventh-day Adventist Church in Croatia, and he said to Nik, "I'm wondering if you would be willing to come and help us. Because you know the language, and you know the situation, we think you would understand. Would you come?"

"The situation" to which the man was referring was warfare between all of the various ethnic groups that had once been a part of Yugoslavia.

The very people who had once played the ethnic card against Nik and his family were now all playing the same card against each other, and thousands were displaced, thousands were being raped and tortured, and thousands were dying.

"The thought had entered my mind," Nik said, meaning the thought that perhaps he should get involved in trying to help bring some humanitarian aid to the people who had driven his family out of their homes so many years earlier. "The thought had entered my mind, but I said, 'Lord, I don't hate those people there. But I'm not sure if I'm enthusiastic enough to go back there and risk my life. There's a war going on there!' "

In a state of shock at what was being asked of him, Nik told the man he needed a few days to think about it.

And think about it, he did. "It took about three or four days—not to get over hate—I didn't have that. But to develop a sense of this is what God wants me to do. And when I came to that point, it was like an experience of freedom. I finally said, 'I can do what others can't. I don't have any sides to take there. I don't differentiate between a Serb, a Croat, a Muslim, somebody Montenegrin or Macedonian. I don't differentiate. It doesn't matter to me. I'll go.' "

Over the course of the next several years, as war continued to rage and ethnic cleansing led to tens of thousands of deaths, Nik made a series of trips to his former home country—the country that had rejected his family because of their ethnicity.

"I traveled to the war zone, but you know, when God asks us to do something, God also provides the means and the protection," he said. "I remember riding in cars through war zones, where we would have to stop. The military would stop us, and they would say, 'Wait, there's too much shelling going on.' And at night—we would travel at night because you could see the tracer bullets easier at night than in the daytime. And so we would stop, and we would watch the fireworks, and then they would subside, and then we would travel.

"I have never been as calm in my life as at that time. I just felt that if God saved me the first time, He'll do it again. So I made seven trips."

That's how Nik found himself in a car with two drunken soldiers who would just as soon shoot him as shake his hand that dark night.

Fortunately, the man who was driving understood the

danger, and he carried all of the conversation with the soldiers. Nik uttered an occasional "Uh-huh," but made sure the men didn't figure out that he wasn't from their part of the country. After about fifteen miles, the men got out, and Nik and his friend breathed a sigh of relief—along with a prayer of thanksgiving!

During those seven trips, Nik saw things that nearly broke his heart. "I remember people in a nursing home. If you could call it a nursing home. It was really a kind of a warehouse with beds. Old people cold, freezing. No heat in that building at all."

Nik had to pause at this point as the emotion of that situation overcame him again. "I cried. Then I called my wife. I said, 'Call my cousins. We need some blankets.' "

I interrupted Nik then. "Nik, those are the people of the age that could have been carrying the guns." I was referring to the guards who had kept his family penned up behind barbed-wire fences in 1945.

"Yeah. But . . . but . . . you—you don't allow a person to freeze to death. You don't do that.

"So we, as a family, collected a fair bit of money and just bought the blankets, and said, 'Cover them up.' You know, even if they're going to die, they need to die warm."

My breath was taken away by that story.

To me, that was one of the greatest miracle stories I've ever heard.

It took a miracle for God to give Nik the ability to forgive the very people who had done so much evil to his family.

We talked quite a lot about that, because I knew that Nik had not only carried humanitarian aid to the people of Bosnia and Croatia, he had also gotten involved in proclaiming the gospel to them.

"Do you hate the people who imprisoned you?" I asked.

"I never have," he told me. He gives a lot of credit to his parents and their generation, who talked a lot about the hard days in Yugoslavia, but never spoke of it with hatred. "They spoke of the horrors of dictatorship, of the horrors of the camp. But they never spoke hatefully. Their attitude was always 'We thank God that somehow He rescued us.'

"So, while I don't have any fond memories of that period, I do have fond memories of a tightly knit Christian family."

"But if you met one of those men who was carrying the gun, threatening your father—could you invite him to receive Jesus?" I asked.

"I would embrace him. I would. Because—you're not inviting the evil person—you're inviting what the person can become. And when Christ comes into one's life, he or she is a new person—totally transformed. You don't recognize the former person."

Nik went on to tell me about one of his cousins whose wife met a former guard in church. He was now a church member, and they embraced and shed tears together.

That, to me, is the miracle-working power of the gospel of Jesus Christ who died to forgive sins—all sins, no matter how heinous—if we will just bring them to Him and let Him bear them for us.

Just before the warfare ended in his home country, Nik, along with his relatives and friends, helped a congregation rebuild their church in the very city where his family had been forced to live in a barbed-wire enclosure. The church is just two blocks from the former site of the camp.

On the day the church was dedicated, Nik spoke to the nearly five hundred people gathered in and around a building designed for two hundred. He told the assembled congregation,

"I pray that this will be a place of justice, where the right thing will always be done in God's name. That people, whoever they are, will be always welcome, no matter what their ethnicity is, no matter what language they speak, that you will always welcome them. That's what God would like this place to be."

Nik's own life of serving those who did not welcome him sets an example of that very type of openness and receptivity.

He's Really Living and helping others get a new lease on real life.

# Converted by a Price Tag

## Doug Batchelor

I've heard a lot of people's conversion stories, but I don't remember talking to anyone else who traces his or her conversion to a price tag.

The price of salvation is infinite—it cost God the life of His own Son, Jesus. But for Doug Batchelor, the price tag that stopped him in his tracks and started him on a path toward God was only $1.19.

And this for a young man who had lived much of his life in a mansion on an exclusive Florida island.

Doug was born into a home in which it seemed that he could have anything he wanted—opportunities, wealth, education. But none of it satisfied him. In fact, he told me that he never started really living until he met Jesus and accepted Him as his personal Savior. And it took a $1.19 price tag to start him moving in that direction—a price tag on a stolen box of whole-wheat pancake mix.

Doug came from a broken home. He says he knows that opposites attract, because his parents were initially attracted to each other, despite the fact that his mother came from a wealthy New York Jewish family and his father was an Oklahoma boy

whose poverty-stricken family fled the dust bowl for California during the Great Depression.

His dad and mom met and married in California. But, as so often happens, the attraction of opposites soon turned to opposite attractions, and the marriage dissolved when Doug was just three years old. After that he couldn't count on being in the same home or school for more than a few months at a time. His mother, an actress who had had small parts in several Hollywood productions, moved back to New York, where she eventually became a film critic for ABC's morning news program *Good Morning America.*

His father, who had become a pilot prior to World War II, started a business after the war, buying surplus airplanes, flying them back to the United States, and leasing them to businesses. Because there were plenty of planes available at dirt-cheap prices, the business prospered, turning him into a multimillionaire who hobnobbed with the likes of Howard Hughes.

Doug could have worked in that business and eventually taken over from his father. "But we were too much alike," he says. "We couldn't get along!"

Both Doug and his father were strong willed; this characteristic in Doug often led to trouble at school. He also suffered from dyslexia and attention deficit disorder. Add to this the fact that when he lived with his father, he had ready access to a liquor cabinet, which a butler regularly restocked. And when he lived with his mother, drugs were available for the asking—marijuana, hashish, and LSD. "Look, Doug," his mother said to him at one point, "I know that you're going to be exposed to drugs eventually. I'd just as soon you do it at home." That's when he began smoking marijuana and hashish with his mother.

It wasn't the kind of environment that you would expect to foster the growth of a strong spirituality.

Which isn't to say there weren't spiritual influences. His mother was Jewish but atheist. Nonetheless, she sent him to Jewish schools, and he studied under rabbis when he was in New York. But when he was with his father in Florida, he found himself sometimes in Catholic schools, sometimes in public schools, and sometimes in military school.

"At the military school, everyone was required to attend worship services on Sunday," he told me. Sometimes he'd go to Catholic services, sometimes to Protestant, and sometimes to Jewish services that were held on Sunday mornings. But he really had no use for religion, especially not for Christianity. His mother had taught him to think of the Bible stories as mere myths and of Christians as hypocrites who persecuted Jews and caused wars.

Doug's restlessness and discontentment with life led him into trouble in more places than just school. He first ran away from school in New York when he was thirteen. It wasn't long till police caught up with him and a friend, but just as quickly as they were picked up, they escaped and hopped a train, hoping to make it to Mexico. "I guess we looked like runaways, though," he says, "because the police soon picked us up again."

At that point, his mother decided Doug was just too much for her to handle, so she sent him to his father in Florida. But that didn't work out well either. There was a stepmother and a stepbrother involved, and Doug didn't get along with either of them. The only solution his father could come up with was to send him to a hotel that he owned. So Doug spent some time there, then finally told his dad he just wanted to be independent.

"I think you're making a big mistake," his dad said. "Look, I've built up this business. You could work for me; you could have everything money can buy. But first, you need an education."

By that time Doug had been in and out of fourteen different schools but only had a ninth-grade education. However, he was ready to take on the world—or so he thought. "I need to find out for myself," he told his dad. And with that, he left home and headed for Boston.

There, separated from family, teachers, and anyone who could tell him what to do, he began living a life of freedom. Because he was only sixteen, he got a forged driver's license that said he was eighteen, then parlayed that into a genuine license that indicated he'd been born two years earlier than he actually had. Documents in hand, he got a job. "I worked as a security guard at night and as a burglar during the day," he confesses.

He explained to me that it's easier to steal things during the day than at night, because if you carry a TV out of an apartment building in broad daylight, people just assume you're moving.

He soon made friends with a Vietnam vet who taught him the skills he needed to begin stealing cars. (Years later, after Doug became a pastor, people knew just where to turn for help if they locked their keys in the car in the church parking lot!)

Doug thought he was enjoying his wild, unfettered life in Boston, but still he knew there was something missing. Despite his atheist, antireligion background, he still felt some sort of hunger—an empty spot in his soul that wasn't being filled.

He had a friend at the place he worked at night who was very religious—but interested primarily in Eastern religions. This friend learned about Doug's "day job" and warned him, "Karma's going to get you, you know!"

By that he meant that what goes around comes around. If you keep stealing from other people, people are going to start stealing from you.

Doug scoffed at such a silly idea. "Look man, I just stole a TV, and nothing bad happened to me."

A few days later, he returned home to find his apartment ransacked and his own TV missing.

It shook him up a little, but he didn't believe there was anything to what his friend had said. Still, Doug started watching how things went. And sure enough, whatever he did seemed to backfire on him in some way. "I'd go out and steal something, but a few days later, someone would steal something of equal value from me. Or I'd get high or get drunk and then go and steal something, but not be able to remember when I sobered up where I'd hidden it."

That's when a $1.19 price tag really rocked his world. "What convinced me that there must be a God was a little thing," he told me. "I was at someone's home, and I stole a box of Krusteaz instant pancake mix, and I did it because, even though I'm using all these drugs, I was a hippie, and I was health conscious, and I did not want regular white pancake mix. This was a whole-wheat variety, and so I said to myself, 'Oh, I've gotta have that.' So I stole it, and I remember on the top of the box it was stamped one dollar and nineteen cents.

"That same day, some friends came through my place. They took my jar of Tang instant breakfast drink. They drank the whole thing. And when I got home, there by the empty jar was the lid that was stamped one dollar and nineteen cents. And I thought, *Oh, this is too much! I just stole this from someone, and somebody took all of mine—it's the exact same price stamp on top.*"

I must have looked at Doug with a little bit of a confusion registering on my face. I guess I was surprised to think that here is a good Seventh-day Adventist pastor, and he seems to be telling me that he believes in karma. So Doug started quoting Bible texts.

"There's some truth to karma," he said. "Even the Bible says, 'With what measure [you] mete, it [will] be measured to you again' [Matthew 7:2, KJV]. *Karma* means basically, 'what you do comes back again.' "

Such a simple concept—but it set him to thinking. It began to pry open the door of his mind to receive spiritual light. Prior to that, he hadn't believed there were any spiritual laws in the universe, and he certainly didn't fall on his knees and give his life to the Lord just because of a price tag. But it opened the door for further exploration.

About that time, his father heard how he was living and decided to make one last attempt at helping his son get his act together. "You still need to finish school," he urged when he flew up to Boston and found Doug. "And I've got just the place. You'll love it!"

"Yeah, right, man," I can hear his hippie son saying.

"You'll love it. Get this: classes are held on two yachts cruising the Mediterranean."

Who could resist the opportunity to go to a school like that? Not even dedicated dropout Doug could.

Within twenty-four hours, his dad had pulled all the strings he needed to, procured a passport for his son, and gotten them tickets to fly to Italy to meet the ships in Naples.

It turned out to be not quite the sort of idyllic life Doug had dreamed of. To him, the ship he was assigned to seemed more like a prison than a school.

In reality, his father had gotten him incarcerated on a yacht with several dozen other young people—the offspring of politicians, Wall Street warriors, and movie moguls—whose parents had sent them there as a last-ditch effort to break them free from cults, drugs, and other demons.

The curriculum was strictly atheistic. Many of the young people on board had fallen prey to religious cults, and their parents wanted them to imbibe some good old humanistic self-dependence. None of this prayer stuff. They were to learn that the way to get ahead is to apply yourself and work hard.

"When I realized what had happened, I began to rebel," Doug told me. "Passive resistance. I wouldn't go to class, wouldn't do my homework, wouldn't swab the decks."

The staff tried everything they could think of—confining him to his room and restricting his meals—but nothing helped. Friends were only too glad to smuggle food to him.

And since he'd decided to pursue spiritual enlightenment, the idea of sitting in his cabin meditating hour after hour didn't bother him a bit.

Finally, the captain took him aside. "What would it take to get you to cooperate?" he asked. "You're ruining morale by not getting with the program."

"Let me go home for Christmas vacation," Doug suggested.

"We were in Tunisia at the time, and the captain went right to the phone, called Florida, woke my dad up, and told him that I was doing so well in the school that they wanted to reward me with a trip home for Christmas!"

Doug kept his end of the bargain, becoming the model student for the rest of his time onboard.

From Tunisia, the ships headed across the Mediterranean for Spain right through the eye of a winter storm. The ships were taking on water, and a mainsail was ripped to shreds. Everyone, right up to the captain, was seasick.

And that's where Doug learned what many atheists do when they think they're going to die. "They pray," he told me. "And it comes very naturally. And I was right in there with them, praying. Even people who don't believe in God have a consciousness of what they're doing wrong. They're making promises to God never to do it again if they get another chance.

"Obviously we survived the storm, and people pretty much forgot their promises. And that's how I learned that fear is not the best motive to serve God. It might be a starting point, but if fear is the motive, when the threat is gone, we often forget our promises.

"That's what happened to me. We got to Spain. I got on an airplane. I ordered a pack of cigarettes and a beer, and I told the teacher, 'You're never going to see me again.' Once they handed me my passport, I reverted to being very belligerent. And I never did go back."

Unaware of the ruse Doug had pulled, his father rewarded him and the rest of the family with a ski trip to Canada. When they got back to Florida and it was time for Doug to fly back to school, he just disappeared again—ran away from home.

He knew where he was going. Once while living with his grandparents near Palm Springs, California, he had discovered a cave. He'd decided he wanted to be a caveman.

But first he had to get to California.

That's how he found himself standing beside a freeway in Oklahoma in the dead of winter, freezing to death with just a Miami windbreaker to protect him from the icy blast that followed every semi that whizzed past.

"It was the lowest point of my life," he said. And yet he wasn't ready to give up on life. And he wasn't ready to give up on his spiritual quest—his desire to find out what life is all about and who God is.

"I knew there was a God. I couldn't figure out any other reason why so many things had happened. I'd come so close to death so many times. I would pull up to a policeman in a stolen car and ask for directions—just so he'd chase us. I'd had so many close calls that I knew there must be a God. So I said, 'Lord, I'm out on Interstate 40 in Oklahoma,' and I said, 'Please, help me! I know I've been a rotten person. But if You'd please help me, I'll try to serve You. I'll try to find out who You are.'

"I said, 'Lord, I need four things. Please help me get a ride to California; please help me get some food, I'm starving; help me get some money.' And I prayed for a ride with someone *normal*. Because I had often gotten picked up by people who were either drunk or high or had ulterior motives. It's risky to hitchhike."

As soon as he finished his prayer, a white van stopped.

The man who picked him up took him all the way to his grandmother's house in Desert Hot Springs, California. He bought Doug food all along the way. When he dropped him off, he handed him forty dollars.

All four of his prayer requests had been answered.

And one more thing.

"I didn't ask God to have someone preach Christianity to

me all the way to California, but that's what he did."

Doug listened to a Christian preach for fifteen hundred miles, but it didn't convince him of anything. He still thought the Bible was a book of fairy tales and that Christians were all hypocrites. "But God kept putting me in situations where I would collide with Christians," he says.

"I realized God had answered all of my prayers, so I decided I would try to find God in nature. My father is part Cherokee, so I decided to try to find the American Indian spirituality in nature."

Doug went very literally back to nature. Maybe you've seen his book *The Richest Caveman.* He took to living in a cave in the Southern California desert—*au naturel.* That is, without any clothes on most of the time.

But he wasn't the first person to take up residence in that cave in Tahquitz Canyon. Someone had been there before and had left a Bible behind. Inside the front cover they had written a note: "I hope whoever finds this Bible finds the same peace and happiness I have found."

Doug wasn't interested. He was a spiritual seeker, but he didn't think there was any wisdom to be found in that old Book.

The Bible sat there untouched for six months. But on his trips into town, Doug sometimes encountered other spiritual seekers. Jesus freaks they called themselves—hippies who had become Christians. And they were quite aggressive in sharing their newfound faith.

Never one to run from an argument, Doug often tried to dissuade them from their beliefs. But he was at a terrible disadvantage. He had no idea what the Bible said.

So finally, he picked the Bible up and began to read. "I got bogged down somewhere in Numbers," he confesses. But then someone told him he should read the Gospels.

After plowing through Matthew, Mark, Luke, and John, he found himself facing a dilemma. He had been amazed at the wisdom he'd discovered in Jesus' words.

But now what?

He realized that Jesus was either a lunatic and a liar, or the Messiah.

"When you live by yourself, you hear spiritually a little better," he says. "I had no radio, no TV, no cell phone. I'd go days without seeing another human. And you just hear that still, small Voice.

"God was telling me, 'I'm really there,' and I realized, *Look, I've tried everything else. I've gone through all these different religions.* I basically discarded Christianity without even trying it because of my prejudice.

"So I got on my knees up in the cave, and I said, 'Lord, if Jesus is really the Messiah, I need to know that. My life is a big zero. Lord, give me some purpose for living. And forgive me and accept me. I've been a real sinner.'"

Doug looked at me earnestly then, and said, "You know, Don. This peace came into my life that you can't explain. People have to experience it for themselves, but it is very real. All of a sudden, at that point, my life changed. I was so excited, I said, 'Lord, I'd like to tell other people what You've done for me in my life.'"

And that's when a particularly amazing miracle happened. Doug's mother was working in Hollywood at the time, and she mentioned to a friend in the TV industry that her son was living in a cave.

Soon the whir of helicopter blades disturbed Doug's peace. But it proved to be an opportunity for him to share what God was revealing to him as television cameras rolled.

You've probably seen Doug on TV. He's on all the time

these days. But that first time was a defining moment in his life, as he saw God answer his prayer to make it possible for him to share his faith with millions of television viewers.

There's more to his story. Doug witnesses for the Lord full time now as pastor of a large church and as the head of a large ministry.

His spiritual journey has been a long one, with many twists and turns. But I for one am thankful for that little $1.19 stamp on top of a box of whole-wheat pancake mix. It started something.

And because of what it started, today a lot of people are hearing the gospel preached; a lot of lives are being changed; and a lot of people are learning to Really Live by giving their lives to Jesus.

Never doubt the power of small things when placed in the hands of God.

---

The entirety of this story can be found in *The Richest Caveman* from Amazing Facts at 800-538-7275.

# Called to Prison

## Carolyn Evans

Carolyn Evans was in prison. By choice. But that didn't make it any less scary. Bewildered, her hands shaking in nervousness and fear, she stood looking around the yard where men, gathered in tight circles, cast ominous glances her way.

She'd finally made it to prison only after putting forth great effort, filling out all the proper forms, and passing inspection. But now here she stood, without a clue as to where to go.

She knew whom she wanted to see, but she didn't know where to find him.

She knew the name of the building she was supposed to be in, but she didn't know where it was.

Casting a nervous glance behind her, she saw two other women coming out of the administration building. One of them was just as nervous as she was—this was her first time in prison as well. The other one was going to a different building, so she just suggested going to one of the guards and asking where to go. Carolyn finally made her way into one of the buildings, where a guard told her how to find the facility she was looking for.

Following the guard's directions, she soon found herself inside a large room where people were sitting at tables, visiting. But she was still bewildered. She looked around for the bars or Plexiglas that would protect her from the prisoner she had come to see. But after observing for a while, she realized that about half of the people in the room were wearing light-blue work shirts and jeans.

The truth slowly dawned on her: she wasn't going to sit behind a barrier, where she would be protected from the hands of the murderer she had come to see. She was going to have to sit right beside him and look him in the eye. She might even have to touch those dangerous hands. And he might touch her whether she wanted it or not.

"What am I doing here? Should I just leave?" she asked herself. No one would be the wiser if she left without visiting the man she had written letters to. She didn't even know what he looked like. And he didn't know what she looked like. He might be in the room right now, and she wouldn't know it. But neither would he know that she had come to visit him. She could escape from prison now. Now was the time! It seemed like a hundred doors had slammed closed behind her on her way in. But those same doors would open for her. The ID she carried with her was her get-out-of-jail-free card.

But this was no Monopoly game. The stakes here were much higher. There was a human soul at risk—maybe even her own.

Carolyn had come to prison of her own free will—sort of.

It wouldn't have been her first choice of places to go, but a few months earlier, she had felt the Holy Spirit speaking to her, reminding her of Jesus' words, "I was in prison and you came to visit me" (Matthew 25:36, NIV).

"I thought, I know someone who is in prison just about twenty minutes from where I live," Carolyn told me. "If I don't go visit him, how can I call myself a Christian?"

You can put that kind of thought out of your mind for only so long before you begin to feel like you're resisting the Holy Spirit. And Carolyn wanted to be sensitive to the Spirit's moving. Finally, she got in her car and drove to the prison. With fear and trembling, she went inside and announced that she wanted to visit a certain prisoner.

"You can't just walk up to the front gate and say you want to visit someone, lady," the man at the front desk informed her. "You have to be on that person's visitor list."

"How do I get on his list?" she asked.

"The best way is to write him a letter and ask to be put on the list."

"But he doesn't even know who I am."

The man behind the desk just shrugged, suggesting, *That's not my problem, lady.*

So Carolyn began corresponding with a man named Anthony,

and eventually, he agreed to put her on his list.

Now she was at the prison, trembling in her shoes at the thought of actually meeting Anthony face-to-face and sitting down at a table with him. Timidly, she approached the female guard who was assigned to the room. "This is my first time here. I don't know what to do."

"Is the man you came to visit in the room?" the guard asked.

"I don't know what he looks like."

"You don't know what he looks like?"

"No."

"Well, why don't you just go find a seat, and I'll have him come to you."

"But he doesn't know what I look like either."

The guard seemed to think this was the oddest thing— why would someone be visiting a perfect stranger? She looked Carolyn over carefully, and finally said, "Well, when he comes in, I'll bring him over to you."

Carolyn hadn't seen this man in more than ten years, and, of course, he hadn't seen her either. But she had a special reason for coming to visit him.

On a day more than a dozen years before, Carolyn was at her desk at work when the phone rang. She still shudders when she thinks of that phone call. Her father was on the line, and she could tell that he was upset. "I have some terrible news," he said. "Yesterday your niece was robbed and murdered."

Carolyn's world instantly turned to fog. "There's nothing you can do to prepare for something like this," she told me. "You always think this kind of thing happens to other people. I guess I screamed when my father told me the news, but I didn't even realize that I had screamed."

Soon Carolyn's co-workers were gathered around her desk, asking how they could help.

That day began a time of intense grieving for Carolyn and her family. When the suspected murderer was caught and put on trial, Carolyn and several others attended the sentencing. Carolyn brought a Bible with her to the courtroom, along with a letter expressing her forgiveness for the accused man.

After the sentence was handed down—twenty years for robbery with a deadly weapon, life for attempted sexual assault, and life without parole for murder—she gave the Bible and the letter to the prisoner's attorney and asked that they be given to the murderer.

She never heard whether he received those items or not, but now she sat in the prison visiting room, waiting to see the murderer for the first time in more than ten years. *How will I react? How will he react?* she thought. *Will he recognize me? Will he turn and stalk out of the room when he realizes a member of his victim's family has come to—what—torment him?*

Carolyn continued to worry. *If he doesn't recognize me and doesn't leave, will I be able to maintain a calm demeanor when I see him? How about when I have to look at those hands that had done that horrible thing?*

It seemed like hours went by—but it was probably only a

few minutes. Finally, she saw him coming toward her. He was a big, scary-looking man. She wondered if she would even have a voice.

"Anthony?" she said.

"Yes."

"I'm Carolyn."

He sat down then, and they visited. She didn't tell him why she was there, just asked him about his family, where he grew up, and where he went to school. She told me that what she had learned helped her better understand the man God had called her to visit. He said he'd never met his father. His mother had been only sixteen when he was born, and he never saw much of her either, and even when she was there, she was usually drunk. His grandfather was an alcoholic.

In short, Anthony hadn't had many chances in life, and, to make matters worse, he had a mental deficiency that still requires regular medication to keep him on an even keel.

Carolyn visited with him for about an hour, and then asked if he'd like her to come back again. When he said that Yes, he'd enjoyed her visit, she promised to return.

When she walked out of the prison that day, the world seemed to be spinning. Her stomach rebelled. She thought she was going to vomit in the parking lot. Visions of those hands—those murdering hands—kept flashing before her eyes. Could she really return and again face the man who had killed her niece?

Yes, by God's grace, she could.

When I interviewed Carolyn, she had been visiting Anthony for three and a half years.

"Did you ever tell him who you were and why you were visiting him?" I asked.

Carolyn told me that before she identified herself to him,

she wanted to know whether she could trust him or not. For ten months she never let on that she even knew what his crime was. One day Anthony told her that his brother was in the same prison and that he had cautioned him against visiting with this strange lady who came to see him. "She's probably either a family member or a journalist," the brother had said.

"Oh, your brother is in prison too? What's he in for?"

"Murder, same as me."

"You're in for murder?" Carolyn asked, playing dumb. "And they let me sit right here by you like this with no barrier between us?"

Anthony nodded his head.

Over the course of several months, Carolyn began to realize that Anthony was truly sorry for what he had done and that he wasn't going to try to deceive her. So, finally, she decided to reveal her real reason for visiting him. One day she said to him, "You know, you've never asked me why I come to see you."

"No, I thought that was just something you did—just came to visit prisoners who don't have very many visitors."

"No, I came specifically to see you, because the woman that you murdered was my niece."

Anthony's head went down. He stared at the floor, his head in his hands. For a long time, he wouldn't even look up. Finally, he raised his eyes, looked Carolyn in the eye, and said, "I am *so* sorry."

"I just started crying," Carolyn told me. "The tears were just flowing down my face."

Then Anthony reached out to her. "Are you OK?" he asked.

"Yes, I'm OK," Carolyn said. "But I've waited for so long to hear you say that."

Then Anthony started trying to tell her what had happened the day that he killed her niece, but Carolyn stopped him. "That's not the reason I'm here. You don't have to tell me what happened. I came here just to tell you that I forgive you and that God offers you His forgiveness."

It was like something that Anthony couldn't even comprehend. He couldn't believe that someone would actually come to him just to offer him forgiveness and tell him that God loves him.

As the visit that day drew to a close, Carolyn stood up and asked if she could give Anthony a hug. "He just looked at me like *You've got to be kidding!*" she told me. "And then those hands that had scared me so badly before, reached around, as if I were his mother, and hugged me."

Carolyn herself had been transformed by her visits in prison. Now, instead of being terrified of those hands, she welcomed them. Now instead of being angry at Anthony, she ministered to him.

But for Anthony, this whole idea of forgiveness was hard to process. He just couldn't understand it. As the reality sank in that this woman who had befriended him was a family member of the woman he had killed, he began to feel worse instead of better. Even though Carolyn was talking to him about forgiveness, it was as though he couldn't forgive himself. "He was so devastated by what he had done, that he tried to hang himself!" Carolyn told me.

"Has he ever been able to forgive himself?" I asked.

Carolyn explained to me that since he's been in prison, Anthony has converted to Islam. She talks to him about Jesus, and how Jesus wants to bear his sins for him, but at this point, Anthony is convinced that Allah can do the same for him.

Things haven't worked out exactly as Carolyn might have hoped. She continues to tell Anthony that her ultimate goal is to see him give his life to Jesus, that she wants him to experience the forgiveness that only Jesus can give, and that someday in heaven she wants to introduce him to her niece.

Anthony listens respectfully, but he's not yet ready to make the step of becoming a Christian. Carolyn continues to visit him and to pray for him, and we'd like to invite you to pray for him as well.

In a development that took place after I spoke on camera with Carolyn, she told me recently that her niece's grandfather had recently written a letter to Anthony, expressing his forgiveness for what Anthony had done.

The next time Carolyn visited him after that letter arrived, Anthony greeted her with a big, warm smile; prior to that she had seldom seen him smile.

As for Carolyn, she's smiling too. She's happy that she responded to the Holy Spirit's prompting and began to visit Anthony in prison. She's had opportunities to minister to many other families of prisoners, as well as the prisoners themselves, in the time that she has spent there. And she can't help but wonder what life would be like if she hadn't gone to prison. Would she be Really Living?

# Set Free in Jesus

## Frank González

As a teenager living in Orlando, Florida, Frank González decided God didn't care about him, so he challenged God, "If You don't care about me, why should I care about You?"

It would take a miraculous revelation of God's love to turn Frank's life around. But when he finally realized how much God loved him, he couldn't stop telling others. In fact, he's led thousands to Christ since that dramatic day.

Frank now serves as the director and speaker of the Spanish-language ministry *La Voz de la Esperanza,* which means "the Voice of Hope." *La Voz* originally was part of the Voice of Prophecy, but today it is a separate ministry. Both of these ministries, which focus on sharing the gospel via radio, the Internet, and evangelistic meetings, are headquartered at the Adventist Media Center in Simi Valley, California.

But if you had known Frank as a little boy, never in your wildest dreams would you have guessed that someday he would be a leading Seventh-day Adventist evangelist!

Not if you had watched him solemnly performing his duties as an altar boy in the Roman Catholic Church in the town where he grew up in Cuba.

Frank was heavily in-
volved in the Catholic
Church because his
mother was a very devout
woman. But Frank takes
after his father's side of
the family much more
than his mother's. And
Frank's father thought
that religion was a waste
of time. He didn't even
believe in God.

A prosperous busi-
nessman during the years
before Fidel Castro took over the government, Frank's father
was at first a strong Castro supporter. But then, as he saw
Castro turning to Communism, Frank's father turned against
the new government. He felt so strongly that the nation was
being led down the wrong road, that he became a leader in a
counterrevolutionary movement.

Those were tough times in Cuba, and families were di-
vided by political rivalries. You didn't know whom you could
trust. Frank's dad managed to keep his revolutionary activities a secret for a time; the Communists knew he was doing
something, but they couldn't pin anything on him at first.
Finally, there came a day, though, when he had to take ref-
uge on his father-in-law's cattle ranch.

Then the soldiers came for him, led by one of Frank's
mother's cousins. They took him away at night, and Frank
would not see his father as a free man again for sixteen years.

Things went from bad to worse for Frank and his mother
after his father's arrest. His mother was a well-educated

woman who had worked for many years as a writer. But now her writing could no longer be published in Cuba. She had to resort to baking cakes to make enough money to survive.

As for Frank's father, the family didn't hear from him for a long time. Later they would learn that for the first forty-seven days of his imprisonment he was tortured mercilessly every single day. Because he had been a leader of the counterrevolution, he knew that if he broke down and talked to the authorities, revealing the names of his associates, many families would suffer. So he resisted. Each day when the guards would take him to the place where he would be beaten, subjected to heat, cold, or whatever was on the agenda for that day, he would fix a picture in his mind—a picture of a little child—a son or daughter of one of the men who had worked with him in the counterrevolution. Then, whatever he was subjected to, his focus would be on saving that little child.

When Frank heard about this years later, it made him think of Jesus—how Jesus took the torture and the pain of the cross, all the while thinking of the souls who needed salvation.

Even though his father was an agnostic at that time, not believing in God, by his courage he still demonstrated an important gospel message.

And in his imprisonment, God reached out to this man who found it hard to have faith.

After forty-seven straight days of torture, Frank's father was ready to surrender. He knew he couldn't take even one more day. He was there in his cell, Frank told me, with rats crawling around him, and he looked up and began to wonder why, if there was a God in heaven, as his wife so fervently believed, He let such terrible things happen to people.

There in his broken state, Frank's father was ready to blame God for what was being done to him, "If You exist like my wife says, how can You be so indolent?" he shouted at the ceiling. "If those two men come to my cell again tomorrow to take me to the torture chamber, then I've had it! I can't resist anymore. I'm going to tell them everything. But the blood of the people who suffer will be on Your hands!"

The next morning, the same two men came to Frank's father's cell. They took him out and led him down the same hallway. But where they normally would turn one way to go to the torture chamber, this day they turned the other direction. Frank's father had been released from torture—not from prison, but from torture.

In the ensuing years, other prisoners were often beaten by the capricious, angry guards for no apparent reason. The person to Frank's father's right and left might be selected and subjected to a merciless pummeling. But his father was never struck by the guards again.

It was enough to make his father think again about his agnostic attitude. Eventually, he became a strong believer in God.

Frank, for his part, continued as a devout believer as a child.

Eventually, he and his mother were able to leave Cuba because his father insisted that they do so, and because the government was only too glad to let dissidents' family members leave. They lived in Spain for a time, then Puerto Rico, then Miami, and finally, they found a home in Orlando, Florida.

By this time, Frank was a young man and was entertaining his own doubts about the existence of God. Because his mother was such a devout woman, he had maintained close contact with the Catholic Church through his growing-up years, usually attending Catholic schools.

He believed in God and in the power of prayer. "I prayed every day, from the time I was four years old until I was about seventeen, for my father to be released from prison," he told me. "But it didn't happen. So, finally I said, 'Well, God doesn't care about me. Why should I care about Him?' So I just edged Him out of my life."

At this time Frank and his mother were living with one of his uncles who had been one of the last members of the family to leave Cuba. While he was in Cuba, he had become friends with a Seventh-day Adventist pastor. In Orlando the uncle discovered that the Cuban pastor's brother was the first elder of the local Seventh-day Adventist church.

Soon the elder was giving Bible studies to Frank's uncle and other members of the family, but Frank didn't want any part of it. "In fact, I took a sort of a sadistic pleasure telling the guy 'No.' I made sure that I was there when he came for the Bible study, so that I could say 'No.' Because it was my way of getting back at God," he confessed.

But that didn't mean he wasn't interested in what was going on. Frank became a proficient eavesdropper, sitting on a couch in the next room, listening to the Bible study.

One day the topic was angels, and the elder told a story about angelic protection and assured everyone there that they had at least one guardian angel with them at all times. Frank found himself laughing at that concept. After all, if everyone had a guardian angel, where was the angel that should have protected his father from being arrested? Where was the angel to open the prison doors and let his father out? Frank decided he didn't believe in angels either.

Until the next day.

"The next day, I found myself surrounded by a gang of thugs," he told me. And even though he's a big man who knows how to take care of himself—he'd learned boxing and judo in Cuba—there was no way he could fight his way out of this situation. There were fifteen or twenty men with chains and knives surrounding him.

"I was there in the middle of the street," Frank told me, "thinking to myself, *Look at all the trouble my dad went through so I could get out of Cuba. And here I'm going to die so miserably, so young.*

"I was still angry at God.

"Then I remembered the story from the day before, about the angel, and I turned to God—silently of course—and I said, *If what that man said is true, and You really care for Frank, I suggest that this is the time to demonstrate it, because I don't think You're going to have another opportunity. But do whatever You want.* I was angry, and I was going to die angry, defiant."

The gang members attacked Frank, and he began throwing punches, trying to defend himself. Then he noticed something very strange happening. "I noticed that even when I missed, they were just bouncing back. They were lunging at me, and as if there was a force that repelled them, they would go back. It happened again and again and again." Finally, Frank's attackers gave up and went away and left him alone there in the middle of the street—pondering what had just happened.

That was just the beginning of a turnaround in Frank's life. It wasn't that he knelt down in the middle of the road and gave his heart to the Lord at that moment; but the next time the elder showed up to give Bible studies, Frank knew he needed to participate. "That was the beginning of my knowing that God cared, that He had a plan for my life, and that Jesus was involved in my life," he affirms today.

Through Bible study, and with careful nurturing from the church elder and others, Frank came to see that God did indeed love him very much. Then Frank sensed that the plan

God had for him included having him share the good news he had discovered with others. He went to college and the seminary, spent years as a pastor and evangelist, and then joined *La Voz de la Esperanza* team as an associate to Pastor Milton Peverini.

Meanwhile in Cuba, Frank's father was finally released from prison in 1979, after serving sixteen years of his twenty-year sentence. Frank told me that Jesse Jackson had to get personally involved in order to get his father released early.

It was a real thrill for Frank to meet his father at the airport in the United States after his release. "It was surreal," he told me. Frank stood and watched his father from a distance for a time, noting that the man's voice sounded just like his own. His gestures were the same. Even though Frank had not been around his father for sixteen years, he could clearly see his father in himself. He uses this observation as an illustration of the way that Jesus wants to reproduce Himself in us when we become His children.

The fact that Frank and his father share the exact same name, as well as a lot of physical characteristics, became a bit of a challenge for Frank a few years later.

In 1994, Cuba changed its stance on religion, abandoning its status as a declared atheistic state, and adopting the terminology "secular state." As soon as that happened, *La Voz* ministry was able to reopen its correspondence Bible school there, and in 1996, Pastor Peverini visited Cuba to participate in a large graduation ceremony in Havana. While he was there, plans were made for graduations to take place all over Cuba in 1998.

By 1998, Pastor Peverini had retired, and Frank had become the speaker and director of *La Voz*. When it came time to apply for religious visas in order to be able to visit Cuba, his staff requested twenty-six visas. A few weeks later, twenty-five visas arrived. Frank's was the only one that had been denied. Frank is quite sure this was because his father's name was still registered as a dissident troublemaker by the government.

But, being the man of faith that he is, Frank decided simply to make it a matter of prayer, and to take the first leg of the trip anyhow, hoping something would change and the visa would be granted. Fortunately, his visa arrived just in time, and he was able to go with his staff to Cuba, where he shared the love he has for Jesus in nineteen cities and witnessed twenty thousand graduates receiving their certificates from *La Voz* Bible schools. In response to his preaching, eight thousand people made decisions for Christ.

A few years later, Frank was able to return to Cuba again and take part in another miracle. For the first time since Communism had taken over that nation, the government allowed the church to rent a government-owned theater for a nine-night series of meetings.

It came about through what the government considers an error, but what Frank knows was a God-ordained miracle. The church applied to be able to rent the theater for nine nights in a row, hoping that maybe they would be granted one or two nights. But when the paperwork came back, the officials had signed off, allowing them to have the theater for all nine nights.

Then, just before Frank was to arrive, church officials went to finalize the plans for the use of the theater. The officials were surprised to hear them talking about nine nights of meetings. "We only granted you one night in the theater," they said.

When the church officials produced the letter, signed by all the right people, the officials were astounded. Apparently, they had thought they were granting only a one-night permit. But because all the paperwork was filled out and signed, the church was able to have the theater for all nine nights!

Frank sees this as an amazing miracle from God. Nothing like it had ever happened before, and it has not happened again.

Enthusiasm for the meetings was so great because of the number of people taking Bible studies that the church had to issue tickets for people to attend. And they had to limit people to attending only one of the nine nights.

The meetings became purely a reaping series. Those in attendance had already studied all of the major teachings of the Bible and were prepared to make a decision for Christ. What a thrill it was for Frank as, over the course of those nine nights, he was able to invite nearly twenty thousand people to give their lives to Christ.

Evangelism, sharing the love of God that he discovered for himself and that his father discovered in jail, is what Frank lives for today. He loves preaching to large crowds, seeing people's lives transformed by the power of the Holy Spirit. For him, he's not Really Living, except when he's sharing the gospel.

# Living on Purpose

## James and Sarah Appel

It is a hot, dry Monday afternoon in November 2006 on the hospital compound in the little village of Béré in Chad, on the southern edge of the Sahara Desert. Dr. James Appel, clad in dirty coveralls, a bandanna tied around his head, is doing surgery with greasy hands.

The patient this day isn't a woman struggling with a breech birth or a baby born with a deformed hand. It's a generator.

Now, I have to confess that I don't know exactly how James was dressed that day. I don't even know exactly what the weather was like. But that's how I pictured it when he described spending a full day working on a recalcitrant machine in hopes that it would help him fulfill his real purpose in life.

When I introduced James and his wife, Sarah, on the *Really Living* program, I spoke of them as "two people who have chosen to lose their life to find it again." James and Sarah are missionaries to the people of Chad in Africa, in what some might consider the old-school way of being missionaries. They live right on a hospital compound, in a two-room house that has electricity only a few hours a day. He's a doctor; she's a nurse. Between them, they supply almost all of the medical expertise available in their village of 15,000 people, and for the 140,000 people living in the surrounding area. Women experiencing difficult births have been known to ride ten to twelve hours in an oxcart to get to their hospital for help.

But on the day I'm telling you about, James wasn't working on a generator to bring power to his house or to the hospital. He was working on a portable generator because he knew it could play a part in introducing Muslims to Jesus on one of the most important days of the Islamic year.

When James graduated from Loma Linda University Medical School, he felt a calling to mission service. In particular, he felt called to go to a little hospital in Béré, Chad. He can't explain it, except to say, "I felt I was supposed to go." He admits that it didn't seem like a smart move. A physician just out of medical school ought to go to a place where there are experienced doctors to work with. But when he heard about the little hospital in Béré, he sensed a call. He told himself, "That's where I want to go!"

Older, more experienced doctors told him not to jump in so fast. But James wouldn't be easily dissuaded. "At least you ought to go take a look at it before you volunteer," his advisor told him. So James arranged to work for three weeks in a hospital in Nigeria at the end of his last year of residency. After that he planned to take a week to visit Chad, which borders Nigeria on the far northeast corner.

When I asked him why he wanted to go to Chad, he described his first visit, which frankly left me scratching my head, wondering why that trip didn't discourage him. Here's how he described the journey: "I was trying to go to Chad for a week, but I got stuck in Cameroon for four days. I missed my first flight from Nigeria to Cameroon. By the time I got to Chad, it was Monday, and I was supposed to leave already on Wednesday.

"I spent all of Monday taking probably the worst public transport ride in the history of Chad. To take the six-hour trip, I left at ten o'clock in the morning, and I was still an hour away by two o'clock the next morning. I was able to go the next day, finally, to Béré on a motorcycle, crossing a river with the motorcycle in a canoe, and got to the other side, to the hospital, and kind of looked around briefly, and saw that it was basically a bunch of empty buildings with a few instruments and medicines lying around. Not much else.

"It was being used sort of as a hospital; there were like three patients in the hospital, and a couple of nurses milling around, and a Congolese obstetrician. But it didn't really look like much was happening."

As I said, that description left me scratching my head as to why a man with a freshly minted medical degree would want to begin his practice there. "In fact," he says, "the mission secretary who was there showing me around, when he put me back on the plane to leave the next day, thought he would never ever see me again."

But the mission secretary turned out to be wrong. The trip to

Chad had only deepened James's determination. "How long have you been there?" I asked him when we spoke in 2007.

"Three years," he replied.

Then I turned to his wife, Sarah, and asked how long she had been there. "Three and a half years," she said.

I knew there must be a story behind that, but before getting to that, I wanted to know why she had given her life to serve in such a remote place. She grew up in Denmark and began her work as a nurse there. But she didn't find it particularly satisfying to work in a hospital in her native country.

One day while Sarah was visiting with an elderly patient, the woman told her that as she looked back over her life, she had few regrets about things she had done. The things she regretted most were the things she had left undone—opportunities she had passed up. Sarah decided she didn't want to have those kinds of regrets. Being young and single, she knew that she had opportunities to do things that might not be available to her later in life. She wanted to make the very best possible use of her nursing degree.

"I wanted to use it where I could make a big difference," she said, "and not just in a hospital where I would be just one in the crowd. It doesn't have to do with me wanting to stand out from the crowd; it has to do with my wanting to feel that what I did was worthwhile—that I could really make someone else benefit from what I have learned."

Her way of making a big difference was to volunteer to serve in a remote hospital in Chad.

James and Sarah actually met in California while they were preparing to go to Africa. "Without actually saying anything to each other, I think we both kind of decided in our minds that it wasn't going to be so lonely in Chad after all," James said with a grin.

And, of course, he was right. James and Sarah were married in a ceremony in Denmark less than two years later.

Life for the young married couple at the mission hospital is not easy, but it's the life they've chosen. If you'd like to know more about their day-to-day lives, James maintains a blog on the Internet. You can easily find it by searching under his name. He's very frank there about the good times and bad.

I asked him if he ever gets overwhelmed. He smiled and said, "Ask Sarah." I turned to her.

"Yeah, he was very overwhelmed when he first came," she said. Sarah had already been working at the hospital for six months when James arrived. "And I guess I was too when I arrived. But I wasn't sure if he was really going to stay."

Apparently, James had a habit of throwing up his hands and saying, "I'm leaving! I can't take this anymore!" And Sarah didn't know whether to take him seriously.

James explained what he was going through. "There are a lot of highs and lows. Then when you're at the bottom of the bottom of the pit, then something happens that renews your strength. God lets something happen that gives you courage, that inspires you to say, 'I know I'm here for a purpose. I know I'm here for a reason.' Yeah, I made a lot of mistakes. Maybe some people suffered and died, but overall, I'm here doing what God wants me to do. And overall I am able to help some people who otherwise would be suffering even more. That's what inspires me. But it's ups and downs. It's not a smooth sail. You're constantly in the valleys and on the mountaintops."

In the hospital, they treat anyone who comes, regardless of religion or even of ability to pay. They do a lot to try to improve the health of people. One thing that was interesting to me was that they have a sliding scale for how much they charge to deliver a baby. If a mother has been in for at least one prenatal visit, a birth costs two dollars. If she came in twice for prenatal visits, the delivery is free. But if the mother hasn't been in for a prenatal visit at all, the cost is five dollars.

The reason for this is that without a preparatory visit, the mother often doesn't know what she's in for when the baby decides to enter the world. With an examination beforehand, the doctor can determine whether the baby is likely to be breech, whether there might be twins, or whether there might be other complications.

James recalled one sad day when a woman arrived at the hospital after a very uncomfortable two-hour motorbike journey on rough roads. Her delivery had begun in her home, but the baby had presented an arm first, and the midwife wasn't able to help. Unfortunately, the baby did not survive the journey; but fortunately, James was able to save the mother's life.

Life is certainly full of ups and downs for anyone serving in a situation like that. But as we visited, James and Sarah shared the excitement that they feel because the hospital recently hired a chaplain. One of the things the chaplain did after joining the staff was begin to invite patients and their families to participate with the hospital staff in morning worship.

Not long after that, a father brought his baby to the hospital. The baby had been born with all his fingers growing together. James managed to separate the fingers and kept the baby there for some time. The father began to attend the morning worship, and when he finally left the hospital, he asked if there was someone who could come to his village and tell them about Jesus.

James mentioned this request in a prayer meeting at the church a few days later, and four teenage boys said they would be willing to go. James and the chaplain began meeting at six o'clock every morning with the boys, praying with them and encouraging them. The volunteers were changed by that experience; they grew from boys who had seldom spoken with God to young men earnestly appealing for divine help in carrying the gospel to a Muslim village.

Meanwhile the church began a fund-raising campaign and managed to raise thirty dollars to help with this mission project. With that money in hand, the young men went to the village and began teaching the people. They set up a church under a mango tree, and, at last report, that church is still meeting on Sabbaths.

And that's not the only village that's been affected. The chaplain often hears requests for someone to come to a new place to teach the people about Jesus.

And that's the real reason—the real purpose—for James and Sarah to live and serve in Chad. They sense that God has called them there to help the people with their health needs, but also to help them with their spiritual needs.

That's also the reason James was doing surgery on a portable generator in November of 2006. The generator hadn't worked properly in over a year. But now James and Sarah had a very special invitation—an invitation to attend a special Ramadan festival in a nearby village. And they had been invited to bring Jesus along with them. A *video* about Jesus, that is.

But if they were going to be able to show the video, the generator had to work.

*Sputter, sputter, sputter.* That's about all James could get out of it. It felt like he had wasted a whole day that could have been better spent in the hospital. Still—and this was no surprise to me—he wasn't ready to give up. With an urgent prayer winging its way toward heaven, he loaded the recalcitrant machine on to the back of the bicycle of the man who had invited him to the village.

The man, Ahmat, was a patient who had come to the hospital and had been treated for tuberculosis. During his two-month recuperation, he had many conversations with the chaplain. And he also got acquainted with James's and Sarah's horses. People in that area are great horsemen.

After his release, the man kept coming back to visit the hospital, the chaplain, and the horses. One day he asked Sarah if he could watch a video. Because there is no electricity in most of the villages, videos are very popular when people get chances to see them.

Sarah selected a video about Jesus. The man watched just a few minutes before going away, but when he came back in November, he invited James and Sarah to his village for the festival at the end of Ramadan—the Muslim month of fasting. "And bring that movie," he said.

So they loaded the generator on the man's bicycle. James and Sarah followed later on horseback, bringing a projector and speakers, and joined in the festivities. Sarah even raced her horse against one of the fastest steeds in the village—and won!

As the sun went down that evening, Ahmat invited the Appels to his house. There they unfolded a sheet, set up the projector and speakers, and pulled the cord on the generator. "It purred for over three hours," James says. And many people from the village watched in wonder as the story of Jesus unfolded before them.

After the video, Ahmat told James, "I understood everything. I know now that Jesus is the Great Teacher."

Getting that message out to people who have never known Jesus as their Friend or Teacher is the purpose for which James and Sarah Appel live. They may not have much of this world's goods, but to me, I'd say they're Really Living. Wouldn't you?

Oh, about the generator. The next time they tried to use it, it wouldn't run.

# Hearing, and Sharing, Voices

## Jim Ayer

Voices are speaking up for God all over the world today. Sometimes they speak to just one person; sometimes to a whole village. Sometimes it seems to be an angel who comes to deliver the message; sometimes the Holy Spirit speaks quietly—or loudly—within a person's heart.

But it's not just angels and the Holy Spirit who are proclaiming the gospel around the world. God likes to use people as messengers as well—in fact, I think that's His preferred channel, don't you?

Jim Ayer thinks so. When we spoke, he said, "Why should the angels get all the blessing of sharing the good news? God wants us to have that blessing too!"

Jim himself has been on both sides of the equation. There have been times in his life when he's been sure that heavenly messengers have been sent to communicate with him. There have also been times when God has used a man or woman to deliver the message. And God has used Jim to share His message with others as well.

Jim can also tell fascinating stories, taken from his work with Adventist World Radio, about how God seems to be

sending angels to remote parts of the earth to get people started listening to the gospel as it is proclaimed by some very human voices.

When you talk with Jim, you know you're talking to a natural-born communicator. I get the feeling that he could sell ice cubes to Eskimos in igloos. He's had the privilege of persuading many people to give their hearts to Jesus. But it took some pretty direct messages from the Lord to get him to the point where he could be used. If you had known him as a young man, you probably never would have expected him to become an evangelist.

When I asked Jim about his early life, his response was quick: "I was a drug addict, a drug dealer, an alcoholic, and a thief. I wasn't the same guy you see sitting here."

He said he went to church as a boy. "But I guess it went in one ear and out the other."

Still, God must have seen something special in Jim, because the good Lord just kept pursuing him until the message of His love stopped going in one ear and out the other, and got caught in Jim's heart and mind.

As a young man, Jim was involved in using and selling drugs. But then one day as he sat alone in a small house, he caught sight of the big picture of the great controversy between

Christ and Satan. And he was surprised to find himself right in the middle of that controversy. The way he described it, he was sitting by himself, smoking marijuana, when all of a sudden it was as if the house expanded into a large auditorium. This was no hallucination; it seemed to be a vision.

Jim could see himself at the top of this auditorium, looking at God and Satan down on the stage, arguing over his soul! As he described it, Satan was using the kinds of arguments that he himself had used to persuade people to begin taking drugs, but God would respond with just a few words that would silence the devil every time.

This went on for some time, and then suddenly, Jim found himself sitting back in that small house all alone once again.

That's when he heard a voice—a voice he believes came from a heavenly messenger. "Jim, you have a short time to decide."

Decide what? Well, he had just seen God and the devil arguing over his salvation. It must have something to do with that. He knew he wasn't living the life he should, but walking away from it would not be easy. He would need strong motivation, and that's exactly what he got.

Every time he did drugs after that he would hear the same voice: "Jim, you have a short time to decide."

He didn't understand what was going on, but finally, he decided that he had to make a change. He promised himself he would never do drugs again. "But you know, Don," he told me, "I found that promises without the strength of God aren't worth making."

Jim managed to stay clear for about eight months, but he said that by that time he so missed his old lifestyle that he found himself crying himself to sleep at night. Finally, one day he gave in and went to a bar. He figured alcohol wouldn't be a bad thing—he'd been worried only about the other drugs. Unfortunately, he met a man at the bar who soon offered him some marijuana, and that brought a quick end to his cleaned-up lifestyle.

But God still wouldn't let go of him. Sometime later, after Jim had married and had a baby boy, he started hearing the voice again. It happened just after he returned from a drug-buying trip. This time, the voice said, "Jim, tonight is your last night to decide."

"It was like the crossroads of eternity were right before me!" he said. "I thought, *Wow!* And I went in, and I went to the drawer, and I got all the stuff out of the drawer, walked into the kitchen, and said, 'Honey, I've got to get rid of all this stuff.' And my wife just looked at me and smiled and said, 'OK.' So I went in the bathroom, and I flushed everything down the toilet."

It wasn't the first time he'd done that sort of thing. It had happened before when there was an unexpected knock at the door. But this time was different. "It was like all of a sudden, all of the cares of my life were lifted off my shoulders. It was so exciting—it was like this huge weight was lifted off me, and I remember—I started to cry. And I looked around, and I looked in the doorway, and there was my wife, and she was crying."

Something from his religious upbringing kicked in about then. "Honey, would you join me in a prayer?" he said, taking his wife in his arms.

"God, I'm sorry it took so long." That was the extent of his first prayer, but he had come under conviction that he needed a spiritual influence in his life to help him get on a better path. He and his wife began searching for a church to attend. They had a friend who was a pastor, so they started attending his church. But soon that wasn't enough. Jim didn't feel that he was being fed. The sermons seemed repetitious, and Jim felt the need of something deeper—some real Bible-based meat he could sink his spiritual teeth into. He got a hold of a Bible and started reading, but he couldn't understand much of what it said.

That was when he saw a television commercial for some Bible Story books. He and his wife had a baby boy by this time, and he knew he didn't want his son to have to go through the sorts of experiences he had just come out of. Maybe if he could teach his son from the Bible, it would spare the boy some of the hard knocks he had been through.

Jim called the toll-free number, and a few days later, a salesman contacted him. "The fellow almost lost the sale," he told me. "Because he wanted to show me what was in the books. I said, 'No, I just want to buy them!' "

When the books arrived, Jim put them on a shelf, waiting for his son to be old enough to read to. But something kept drawing his eyes toward that bookshelf, and finally, he took a volume down and started reading. "Don, they were so exciting—they were wonderful—they explained the Bible on a level I could understand, and this was just the meat I had been needing."

Jim told me just how seriously he took what he was reading. As he read through the stories about the Old Testament sanctuary system, he began to think that he needed to find a lamb to sacrifice to make atonement for his sins. But how could he do that? People would think he was crazy. Still, he was willing to do it.

That's when he met Jesus. Still reading in the Bible Story books, just as he was ready to go purchase a lamb, he said, "I got to volume nine." A relieved expression came over his face as he talked with me. "And it explained that Jesus Christ is the Lamb slain from the foundation of the world. And I thought, *Hallelujah! Praise God! I don't have to go kill a lamb! Jesus is my*

*Lamb!* And at that moment I fell in love with Jesus Christ. It was just the most exciting thing that you can imagine."

As a side note, Jim told me that a few years later he took a job selling those very same Bible Story books, and at a meeting he attended, people were commenting about the television advertisements they had spent money on, saying that they had been a big waste because only one call had ever come in response to the ads. Jim stood up and said, "I was that one call!"

Jim testifies, "I have no question in my mind. No question, God loves us so much, He will go to the ends of the earth to touch us and lead us and guide us."

Having read through the entire Bible Story series, Jim knew that there was a lot more depth to the Bible than what he was hearing in church. He and his wife began visiting a lot of different churches, but each time he would find something that the pastor said that he knew wasn't biblical, and then they would move on to another church.

They were searching for God, and, at the same time, I believe God was trying to reach them. And that brings up an interesting question: Does God ever use toothaches to speak to us?

I'm not sure how you would answer that, but in Jim's case, he found himself with a toothache that led him to a deeper understanding of the Bible. As he asked around town about dentists, people told him about one man who was "a real religious nut." To Jim that sounded interesting, so he called up and made an appointment.

"You never want to ask a dentist, when he's got your mouth crammed with cotton, what he believes," Jim says. For forty-five minutes, while the dentist worked on his tooth, he talked to Jim about the Bible. And everything rang true! These were the things that Jim himself had been studying in the Bible.

When he was finally able to talk again, Jim asked the dentist which church he went to. "Seventh-day Adventist," he replied.

What a disappointment! Jim had heard of "those crazies" before. He wanted nothing to do with them. Still, the dentist invited him to stop by church sometime and told him that they met on Saturday not Sunday.

Saturday, not Sunday? It almost sent him reeling. He and his wife had been discussing that exact point recently. In their own Bible study, they had noticed that the Bible always referred to the seventh day—Saturday—as the Sabbath.

Jim knew he had to go and check this out for himself. He had been going from church to church to church, carrying a notepad with him, writing things down as he listened to the sermon, then going and researching in the Bible to find out whether the pastor agreed with the Bible or not. So far he hadn't found one that did.

This time it was different, though. Jim checked out the things the pastor was saying and found them to be biblical. Soon he and his wife were attending regularly, and before long, they were baptized members. But not just pew-sitting members, they were active: preaching, giving Bible studies, and sharing the good things they had learned from the Bible.

After a while, though, that first love experience wore off, and Jim began to feel that although his life was better than ever and he was having great success in his business, once again, there was something missing. This time, though, he wouldn't turn to drugs or alcohol to fill the void. Instead, he and another man decided to start a Bible-study group.

At the first meeting, the leader informed the group that everyone there needed to commit forty-five minutes per day to Bible study and prayer if they were to be part of the group. Commitment forms were passed around, and Jim stared at the bottom line all through the meeting. Then at the end, as the group watched a video presentation, Jim heard the preacher speaking directly to him: "You know, in your life you pile up so many things that even if the Holy Spirit of God called you, you couldn't even answer."

Tears filled Jim's eyes as he considered the man's words. When the lights came back on at the end of the video, he dried his eyes, stared at the line for a moment longer, and then signed it. "And I found those forty-five minutes," he told me. "I found those forty-five minutes because the Holy Spirit spoke to me, and I turned off all the premium channels on television. I actually found an hour, sometimes I found two hours.

"And praise the Lord, he brought my wife right along at the same time, and the two of us began studying and praying together and getting so excited!"

The next time Jim heard a voice, he sensed the Holy Spirit was telling him that God wanted him to become more active in doing things for the sake of the kingdom of heaven. He discussed it with his wife, who suggested that they go on a Maranatha trip. Maranatha is a group that organizes volunteers to travel all over the world to build churches, schools, orphanages, and other buildings in countries where needs outstrip resources.

Within weeks Jim found himself building a cinderblock wall with a group of volunteers in Venezuela. This time it was a human voice that spoke to Jim: "Isn't it wonderful that we are the answer to so many people's prayers?" said a man who was working with him.

For Jim, the answer was an enthusiastic Yes!

Getting involved with Maranatha inspired Jim and his wife so much that they knew they needed to do it again and again. Within a few weeks, after returning from Venezuela, they led a group to Honduras to finish building a school. And in the ensuing years, they have traveled to many more countries, not only helping with building projects but also with health projects (Jim told me he's even learned to extract teeth while helping a dentist), and preaching the gospel.

Sharing Christ with others is the greatest thrill Jim has experienced in his life. "Without Jesus Christ, people just can't understand what living really is," he says. "But when you have Christ in your life, that's really living, I mean, and you share it with others. To me there is nothing like standing before a crowd and sharing Jesus Christ and seeing people respond to the power of the Holy Spirit. It's not you. But it's so wonderful to be the vehicle through which He speaks. . . . There isn't living aside from that, in my mind."

Today Jim works full time spreading the gospel with an organization whose mission is to carry the words of Jesus and the love of Jesus to parts of the world where missionaries may not be able to go. Adventist World Radio (AWR) has studios and radio stations strategically located around the globe to broadcast gospel messages prepared by local speakers in more than seventy major languages.

And it's not just Jim who is receiving special communications from heavenly messengers these days. He told me fascinating stories about mysterious strangers appearing in villages, asking to speak to the chief, and showing the chief where to find AWR broadcasts on a radio, then disappearing. This is in an area where any missionary who would venture into a village would be shot on sight.

There were a lot more stories in the interview that I did with Jim, but the upshot of it all is that you can try all kinds of things in your life, whether drugs, alcohol, or entertainment, but the thing that really makes life fun and exciting is knowing Jesus and sharing Him with others. To Jim, and to me, that's Really Living!

# Faith as a Little Child

## Miroslav Kis

"Mom, I'm not going to school tomorrow, even if the teacher kills me!"

Miroslav Kis was only in the second grade when he burst into his mother's bedroom in the middle of the night with that defiant proclamation.

He found his mother awake, on her knees beside her bed, praying for him.

That was no surprise. He had often seen her in prayer. But what might surprise you is how Mrs. Kis responded.

Miroslav Kis (pronounced *Keesh*) was born in Yugoslavia at the height of the Second World War. He was the tenth of eleven children born to faithful Seventh-day Adventist parents in a tiny village that boasted a church of more than a hundred members—the only Adventist congregation for many miles around. Miroslav's grandparents and parents had been instrumental in raising up the church after his grandfather took Bible studies from a colporteur.

"We were a poor family," he told me. But few of us have ever experienced poverty on the level that Miroslav did. On January 31, 1945, just as the war was drawing to a close, his

father was killed. And then, after the war was over, things didn't get better for a long time. "I can remember being so hungry I would jump up and down on the bed to try to relieve the pain," he said.

Most of his older brothers and sisters were already out of the home by that time, and were able to fend for themselves to a certain extent. But Miroslav and his younger sister bore the brunt of the postwar hardships. Their mother was able to provide only one meal per day—a single slice of bread and some onion soup.

"It wasn't because we didn't have land to farm; it was because the land was still filled with unexploded bombs and land mines," he explained. He was so thin and so weak that several times the local physician had him admitted to the hospital just so he could have food three times a day. That went on for three years, almost up to the time when Miroslav was ready to begin school.

When he did begin school, his first-grade year was challenging, but because he had the same teacher that his mother had studied under many years earlier, he got a certain amount of understanding for the peculiar belief system that caused him to be absent every Saturday. As long as he did his homework and knew the lessons that had been taught on Saturday, everything went fine.

Miroslav's second-grade teacher wasn't so understanding. Although he was the son of the first-grade teacher, he seemed to be perpetually angry. Students were treated like army recruits at boot camp. In slightly broken English, Miroslav described a day at school this way: "When teacher comes in, in the morning, you stand up at attention. You step out of the place where you are sitting—we were sitting two by two—you step out, you stand at attention. He looks all over us. He takes his book, he calls the roll, and when he is done, then he says, 'Sit!' He never spoke to us personally. When he would tell us something, the only response is 'Yes, sir!' "

Not only was the teacher a strict disciplinarian, he also expected flawless scholarship. "We had to know all our lessons all the time. He could call, and he could ask anybody from any months—three, four months before, some aspect—and if you didn't know, then if he is in good mood, then he will take a stick and hit us here." Miroslav showed me the palm of his hand. "And it leaves marks. If he was very angry, then he would give it on our back. But if he was absolutely enraged, then he would hit us with stick on our nails. And that hurt so much that you cannot cry, you cannot scream."

As you can imagine, little Miroslav was terrified of his teacher and was anxious to do anything he could to stay out of trouble. At first he managed to keep the peace by getting assignments from other students and making sure that by Monday morning he had absolutely mastered whatever had been taught on Saturday.

Then one Monday, after roll call, the teacher stared right at him and announced "Kis! I want to see you in class next Saturday!" Tuesday morning, the same thing. Wednesday, the same. And all the poor boy could do was say, "Yes, sir!"

That evening he told his mother what was going on.

In postwar Yugoslavia, people were guaranteed religious freedom, but along with that freedom came the rule that parents couldn't force their children to follow their ancestral faith. "You know I cannot tell you what to do," his mother said. She knew that if neighbors found out she had told her son not to go to school on Saturday, she could be accused of brainwashing him. One night she would just disappear from the home, and it might be months before her children would find out what had happened to her or whether she was dead or alive. "It must be your decision, son. You have been going to church. You have listened to sermons. You know many psalms by heart. You know so much. You don't need me to tell you what God wants. You need now to make that religion to be your own."

Thursday and Friday the teacher drove the point home again. Kis had better be in school on Saturday—or else!

Friday evening at prayer meeting, everyone at church knew what was going on at the school, and everyone prayed for Miroslav to have the courage of Daniel, to stand for the right no matter what the danger.

The multitude of prayers brought new courage to the boy, but still by Saturday afternoon, he was beginning to feel the pressure. After all, it wouldn't be the prophet Daniel or Joseph or any of the other Bible heroes who would have to face his cruel teacher on Monday morning. "And I am not Joshua, to say to sun to stop!"

Sunday morning the pieces of the teacher's plot against

him began to reveal themselves. He knew that because Yugoslavia's constitution guaranteed all people the freedom to live according to their religion, he couldn't punish Miroslav for skipping school to attend church on Sabbath. But Miroslav could be punished for not knowing his lessons.

When Miroslav began going to his school chums, asking them to tell him what assignment had been given the previous day, not a one of them would tell him. Under the threat of severe consequences, they had been forbidden to help their friend.

It was a long, lonely walk to school on Monday morning. Fear tied the little boy's stomach in knots. None of the other children would speak to him, or even look at him. Looking at the school building, he felt like Daniel at the mouth of the lions' den. Was there a God in heaven who could close the mouth of the human lion inside? Or was he about to be devoured?

As soon as the teacher had ordered his students into the classroom and told them to sit, he began going from child to child, testing their knowledge of Croatian personal pronouns—a topic he had first introduced on the Sabbath while Miroslav was at church.

Most lessons in the school were taught in Ukrainian, Miroslav's first language, but students were required to know Croatian as well. Because the church's Bibles and hymnals were in Croatian, Miroslav spoke the language fluently. But as a second-grader, he had never heard of such a thing as a personal pronoun.

When he couldn't recite properly, the teacher had him stretch out on a bench at the side of the room. In his hand was the stick he used to punish students who didn't know their lessons.

"I was very poor, and always hungry, and very skinny," Miroslav reminded me. "I had upholstery, but I didn't have padding."

There is a twinkle in his eye when he tells the story today, but there was no humor that day in the classroom. The stick came down on his back one, two, three, four, five, six, seven, eight, nine, ten! And then he was sent back to his seat.

The teacher went on with the drill, and soon he was back at Miroslav's desk. Again to the bench—one, two, three, four, five, six, seven, eight, nine, ten blows! Back to the desk, back to the bench. Over and over again. By the fifth or sixth time, Miroslav was beginning to catch on, and he managed to guess the right answer. But then the teacher changed his strategy, tripping him up again.

Other children in the room, witnessing what was being done to their friend, began to sob, and as soon as they would let the slightest sound come from their mouths, they, too, would be punished.

"I lost count," Miroslav told me. "But the other students said that I was beaten with ten blows nine times that day."

Finally, after the ninth time, as the teacher approached again, Miroslav's seatmate took his life in his hands and shouted at him, "Run, stupid!" and Miroslav took the advice.

Up out of his seat he jumped and ran out the door. He was small but quick. The teacher was instantly on his trail, chasing him down the street—a large man with long legs, he was gaining on the boy, but the boy was quicker and would dodge away each time the teacher almost caught him.

On the street people could see what was going on, and soon they began to cheer for the underdog, encouraging Miroslav to keep running. Realizing what was happening, the teacher finally gave up in embarrassment and stalked back to the school.

Miroslav, for his part, limped home. His mother, seeing that he didn't have his books and that he was crying, hugged him and kissed him on his forehead, but didn't ask any questions. When a neighbor girl brought his books to him that afternoon, she said nothing about what had happened in school.

When it was time for bed, Miroslav tried to undress, but his underwear was glued to his back by dried blood.

He spent a miserable night lying on his stomach, trying to sleep, and awoke in the morning with a fever. By ten o'clock that morning, his mother could see that something was seriously wrong, but he still hadn't told her what had happened at school.

"We're going to the doctor," she announced, then went out to hitch their horse to their wagon. Still unaware of Miroslav's condition, she seated him on a plank beside her and began the ten-mile trip to another village. The boy must have suffered terribly as they rode over bumpy dirt roads.

Imagine what the last six miles—on cobblestones—must have felt like!

"Somehow we arrived," is all Miroslav could say as he described finally getting to the doctor's office. I'm sure much of the agony of that trip must be mercifully faint in his memory by now.

The doctor was a kind, older gentleman who sometimes came to the school to teach the children about hygiene. He examined Miroslav, taking his temperature, checking his throat and ears. He then said, "Take off your jacket."

"No."

"Take it off," his mother said.

Miroslav looked at the doctor, tears in his eyes. "Can my mom go out for a minute?" he asked.

The doctor looked at his mother. She nodded, a puzzled look in her eyes, and stepped out of the room.

When the jacket came off, the doctor gasped. "When did she do this to you?" he asked kindly.

"No! No!" Miroslav said. "Not my mother. The teacher."

"The teacher?"

"Yes!"

"Lie here on the table, on your stomach."

Slowly, painstakingly, the doctor began pulling Miroslav's underwear away from his beaten and bruised body. Dried blood came with it. In places where the teacher's rod had struck bone, the skin was completely beaten through, and the doctor found it impossible to stop the bleeding.

Finally, he went to the door and asked Mrs. Kis to come in. She screamed when she saw her son's condition.

"No time for that," the doctor said. "You must be my nurse and help me treat your son, but no one else must know."

"Why didn't you tell me, son?" she asked.

"You have enough trouble of your own without worrying about me," he replied. "I didn't want to trouble you."

Together the doctor and his mother patched him up as best they could with bandages, finally managing to get the bleeding stopped. Then there was a tetanus shot and antibiotics.

When it was time to go home, Mrs. Kis went to a neighbor's house to borrow some hay. She put some on the seat of the wagon and some on the floorboards, and Miroslav was able to kneel and lay his head on the seat. He slept all the way home.

Tuesday and Wednesday passed in a blur of pain and fever. Finally, by Thursday Miroslav was well enough to go back to school. The teacher came in, looked the children over, and then looked at Miroslav. "Kis. It's OK. I understand."

Friday was the same. But a seven-year-old boy's mind didn't know who to trust. He knew he couldn't stand another beating. "It was good for prophet Daniel, but I don't know if it's good for me," he told me as he recounted the terror he had felt.

"Mom, I'm going to school tomorrow," he said when he arrived home that Friday afternoon.

"She hugged me, and she said, 'I will love you like any other brother or sister. You do what your conscience tells you, and no one in the village, in the church, or in the home, will tease you. Feel absolutely free to act your conscience.' "

Word of Miroslav's decision spread through the church at prayer meeting that night, and everyone began to pray fervent prayers, "Lord, give him courage!"

But for every prayer for courage that ascended, a counterprayer went up from a little boy in the congregation. It was easy for a shoemaker to pray for the boy to have courage—on Monday he would be repairing shoes. On Monday the boy would be facing the wrath and rod of a man who had already beaten him bloody.

Miroslav left the meeting still convinced that he had no choice but to attend school on Sabbath.

Then came the dream. In it Miroslav saw a wall, and in front of the wall, a finger waving back and forth as if to say, *Don't do it!* As he watched, an arm became visible, then a face. Trembling so hard that he could hear his bed squeaking, he peered at the face, desperate to wake up from what he knew was a dream, but also desperate to know whose face it was. He could see sadness in the expression, but he couldn't tell who was sad.

"Then I saw the wings on the back," he told me. "And I realized it was my guardian angel. I realized my angel was sad.

"I'm not going to school, even if he kills me!" he said in his dream. And in speaking, he woke himself up.

Up and out of bed, Miroslav ran to his mother's room. "I'm not going to school, even if he kills me!" he announced as he bounded in.

His mother, on her knees, praying for him, raised her hands to heaven and said, "Lord, thank You for answering my prayer so quickly."

As you can imagine, the rest of the weekend passed very slowly. On Sunday he went from house to house, asking schoolmates to tell him the previous day's assignments, but not only did the children refuse, some of their parents scolded him for being so stubborn and making so much trouble.

Monday morning a trembling, fearful boy stood all alone beneath a chestnut tree in the schoolyard, waiting for the summons to the lions' den.

The principal came out of the school and called first and third grade to come in, then fifth and sixth. Then he announced that there would be no class for second and fourth grade that day.

Tuesday it was the same.

But Wednesday the classes were called into their room. Miroslav's wounds were nearly healed by then, and it terrified him to think that just when he could finally sit down comfortably again, he would receive another beating.

But his teacher didn't come into the room. Instead, the

principal came in and announced, "Yesterday, your teacher was sentenced to three years in prison for abusing Kis. Seven of your parents and the physician sued him. His teaching license is revoked for life. There will be no classes until you are called back. You will have a different teacher then."

Suddenly, the village outcast was the town hero. And a boy who had exercised the faith of a little child had learned to know his God as a personal Friend.

There's more to the story of Miroslav's life. There's the story of his time in the army, how God helped him get an exit visa so he could study theology in France, and how he became a professor and professional ethicist. He's writing his own story, and I'm sure you'll enjoy reading his book when it is published, but let me share just one more part of the story—the part where he explained to me what his childhood sufferings taught him and how they still color his life today.

I'll let him tell it in his own words.

"I told this story, and some other stories in one of the academic, professional lectureships, and when I finished, according to the procedure, one person responded to what I said. And in a very polite way, he said that I was a legalist, because God would never expect that from anybody.

"Against protocol, the person in charge asked, 'Do you want to respond to the responder?'

"I said, 'Yes. I have two things to say. First of all, no one of us has ever the right to say who is a legalist, because that's the issue of motives, and no one of us can judge motives. Second,' I said, 'here is chapter twelve of Hebrews, following chapter eleven, which says, Here is this great cloud of witnesses. So let's lay down the weight—and so on. Verse two, "Looking to Jesus the pioneer and perfecter of our faith"

[NRSV]. How about Daniel, how about the three Hebrew worthies, how about Joseph, how about Jesus? Were they legalists too? And then, he says, "Who for the joy that was set before him endured the cross, despising the shame, and is seated at the right hand of the throne of God. Consider him who endured from sinners such hostility against himself, so that you may not grow weary or fainthearted." ' And then I underlined this one, and I said, ' "In your struggle against sin you have not yet resisted to the point of shedding your blood" ' [ESV].

"And then I concluded. I said, 'And I have shed my blood.' And clapping came from the people that were listening.

"Every day I challenge God to come through in my life, as my God. . . . Whatever I'm facing, I'm saying to God, 'Listen, I'm at the end of my rope. But You prove that there is still rope, because You still exist.' "

The faith of a little child still lives on in this man of God more than sixty years later. And it still reaches out and touches others, pointing them to the God who helped a little boy and providing the support they need to stay strong through their own personal trials.

Miroslav Kis is Really Living, and he's been doing it since he was a tiny, nearly starved boy in Yugoslavia.

# Where There's a Well, There's a Way

## Lynn and Gary Bartholomew

I was shocked when Gary Bartholomew told me that fifteen thousand people die every day, either from a lack of water or from waterborne diseases. Most of the people in the world don't have the luxury of clean water flowing from a tap in their homes.

Yes, that's right, I called it a luxury. You and I may take it for granted that when we turn a handle good, clean drinkable water is supposed to flow into a sparkling glass that's been sterilized in our household dishwasher.

But for the people living and working at one of our Seventh-day Adventist vocational schools in Guatemala, clean, safe drinking water was completely out of their reach.

Oh, yes. They had water in their taps. But it was water pumped from a nearby river. A few years before, that water had been clean and safe to drink. But nowadays many more people are living upstream than there used to be, and those people use the river not only for drinking water but for sewage disposal. Today, the river flowing by the school is loaded with pathogens and parasites.

That problem came to the attention of brothers Lynn and

Gary Bartholomew several years ago. They had made several trips to Guatemala to help with a variety of projects at the school, and they had become aware of the problems with the water. But "what kicked my pockets," Lynn told me, "was a hepatitis outbreak at the school, and at the nearby orphanage also run by the church."

Some strains of hepatitis are spread through water. Contracting these strains is totally preventable by avoiding contaminated water.

But that's easier said than done in an area of Guatemala where there are no wells and no well-drilling equipment.

Lynn and Gary Bartholomew know something about wells. They grew up in a family of well drillers. They aren't in that business anymore, but they both still deal with wells. Lynn has a business specializing in well rehabilitation—helping people get more water from their wells—and Gary is an electrician who installs pump systems and services pumps.

The brothers had been to Guatemala many times, and the water situation concerned them deeply. They'd made it a matter of prayer, but the hepatitis outbreak convinced them that maybe they needed to do something else.

After being "kicked in the pockets," the brothers decided the best thing to do would be to hire a Guatemalan well driller to try to find safe water for the school. Seven months and twenty thousand dollars later, the local man had managed to drill a two-hundred-feet-deep well. But the water coming from it was muddy and contaminated with ground water.

"We felt that was a failure," Gary told me.

When the brothers investigated further, they found that the local man was using outdated drilling methods that would never produce a good well. And that was when they decided they would have to get directly involved.

When you sit and talk with Lynn and Gary, they radiate joy as they tell you story after story of miracles God has worked to help them provide safe drinking water for people.

There were many obstacles to overcome before they could start drilling for water in a country on the far side of Mexico. First of all, they needed equipment. Then they needed to find a way to get the equipment to Guatemala. Then they would have to get it through customs. And even if they could do that, they had no reliable information about the geology of the area where they needed to drill. Would they find water— or just a dry hole?

But where they had only questions, God had a whole list of answers. They tell me that they take no credit for what happened next. There's no way they could take credit for it because they see the fingerprints of God all over everything that happened.

Take, for instance, getting their first drill. Since neither of them is in the drilling business anymore, they didn't have any equipment they could send to Guatemala. But they do belong to well-drilling organizations. Now, they'll admit that the drilling community doesn't have much of a reputation for being softhearted do-gooders. In fact, they're generally regarded as a pretty rough bunch. They have to be tough, considering the type of work they do.

But the brothers put out the word around a drilling organization in the Pacific Northwest that they were looking for equipment to use in Guatemala. "We were thinking that maybe a Bucyrus Erie 22W would be the right size drill to do our work down there," Gary said. And then he continued, "One Friday night, the phone rang about ten o'clock, and this was in August. We were planning to go that winter, and the fellow on the other end said, 'Gary, our family has a 22W Bucyrus Erie well drill. It's been in the family, it's been well kept, and we believe it's good for fifty more wells. What would that do for your project?'

"I was asleep when I answered the phone," Gary says. "But that woke me right up!"

And that was just the beginning. Offers of equipment poured in from all over the Northwest. But, of course, they needed a truck to be able to haul all of it. "I have a tractor and lowboy you can use," one man offered. So Lynn headed for central Oregon, towing the lowboy. And because he was driving unfamiliar equipment, he took along an infrared gun to be able to keep tabs on the temperature of all the axles, the differential, and the transmission.

It didn't take long before he noticed that one of the axles on the lowboy was dripping oil. So he stopped and had a mechanic work on it and put it back together. "That lasted for thirty miles," he told me. Then the axle started slinging oil all over the road again.

But Lynn was doing the Lord's work.

He didn't expect a miracle, but he got one anyhow.

There was no way he could keep oil on that axle, so he kept stopping and checking the temperature. He can't explain it (except to say that he believes in miracles), but that axle ran twenty degrees cooler than all the other axles all the way to Oregon and back!

Then there was the matter of getting all their equipment safely shipped from Spokane to the school in Guatemala. They both knew that trying to get a large truck plus a shipping container full of tools through customs could be more than challenging—it could be downright dangerous. They had heard horror stories of contractors who had ended up in jail on some trumped-up charges while trying to get construction equipment into Central American countries. And while they were in jail, their equipment mysteriously disappeared, never to be seen again.

So it was with much prayer that they sent their shipment south to Houston, Texas, where it was to be loaded on a ship for its journey to Guatemala.

This was one of the places where they saw the fingerprints of God. "I bought tickets to go down there in October," Lynn said. "And the last of the equipment got there the day before we got there in January. And there wasn't a single piece missing, and there had been no trouble clearing customs."

The equipment they use to drill wells in Guatemala isn't exactly the most up-to-date high-tech stuff available—not by a long shot. But high-tech equipment is expensive to buy and expensive to maintain. They're perfectly content with their antiquated drill rig. You can almost fix it with bamboo if something breaks, they say.

And there's another advantage to using the old, slow drill.

It gives them time to get acquainted with the people they are helping and to introduce the people to Jesus. "This isn't about water," they tell me. "It's about Jesus."

Their first well project was on the campus of the school. They had no idea where would be the best place to drill or what sort of obstacles they would encounter on the way to fresh water, but they soon found out.

Before a good, steady flow of clean, drinkable water came bubbling up, they had drilled 350 feet straight down through solid rock!

When they told me that, I realized that there's a good reason why the people in the area can't dig their own wells. It takes some real expertise and some very specialized equipment to dig a hole that deep!

And it takes more than digging a hole to create a functioning water system. It takes know-how and just the right kinds of valves.

That became another problem that they'd need a miracle to solve.

It was on a Friday when they finished making preparations for hooking their well and pumps up to the school's water pipes. And that was the day they discovered they were missing two essential valves.

It would take ten days to get the valves from a supply house clear across the country. So, the whole project would have been delayed for another week and a half, except that that very afternoon a man who was straightening things up in the shop on campus came upon two valves that exactly fit the bill.

And then, as if to confirm that this had all been happening on God's timetable, within a few minutes after the new well was hooked into the campus system, the transformers supplying power to the pumps down by the river blew up.

The whole campus would have been without water if the right valves hadn't been installed on time.

But more important, Lynn and Gary saw this as evidence that the Lord was leading in a special way. "It's been one of the biggest blessings you could ever hope for," Lynn said. "Because I never want to see another drop of water out of that river on that campus!"

With clean, pure, safe drinking water flowing through the pipes, things have been changed for the better at that school and in the orphanage next door. In the first year alone, health care costs declined by 70 percent!

And soon people in surrounding villages began to take note of the changes. And they began to request wells for their villages. Lynn and Gary continue traveling to Guatemala every winter, and now they work out in the villages. It takes about three weeks to drill a well, and during that time they make friends with the villagers.

And they do more than provide drinking water—they bring the Water of Life with them as well.

Recently an eleven-year-old boy from their home church went with them and held a full evangelistic series in the village where they were drilling. He drilled down into the hearts of the people, introducing them to his best Friend, Jesus; and at the end of the series, several people were baptized in the clean, fresh water flowing from the village's new well!

"I didn't know what I was getting myself into," Lynn says about his decision to begin drilling wells in Guatemala. But he's never regretted getting into it.

Because he knows that in bringing water and the Water of Life to people, he's Really Living!

# Living in Other People's Shoes

## Carl and Teresa Wilkens

How does a good Christian missionary get to the point where he can work side by side with a gang of machete murderers when the blood on their hands—literally *on their hands*—has hardly dried?

Carl and Teresa Wilkenses' life together has been an adventure that has taught them a lot of things—things you'd never expect to learn as Christian missionaries. And it continues to be an adventure as they travel all over the United States, often by bicycle, sharing with young people the important lessons they've learned in a life of serving others. When I talked with them in Southern California, they were on the last leg of a 1,600-mile ride from Spokane to Los Angeles via Seattle and San Francisco.

After graduating from college and getting married in 1981, Carl and Teresa landed at their first overseas post of Zimbabwe just six weeks after their nuptials. Carl had done a stint as a student missionary while in college and had fallen in love with Africa. So when he proposed, Teresa was aware that life with him would probably involve service outside her own country.

With a wink, I asked Carl whether he proposed to her with the

stipulation that she had to say Yes to Africa as well as to him. "Anywhere in the world" was what the proposal included—or at least implied—Carl said. "And she said Yes," he added with a smile.

But adjusting to life in a foreign country was no piece of wedding cake for Teresa. "The hardest thing for me was security issues," she told me. "I'd never really lived outside the U.S., and coming to a country that had just gone through guerrilla war where white-skinned people were targeted was very scary for me. Sadly, another missionary couple had been killed just a few months before our arrival."

The difficulty of adjusting to life as a newlywed in a new country was almost too much for Teresa. "That's what led to my get-me-out-of-here moment," she told me.

But looking back on that time now, having gone through another very serious get-me-out-of-here moment when she actually did have to flee for her life, she realizes that those early experiences in Zimbabwe served a purpose. They were preparing her to face later trials with faith and courage, keeping her hand in the hand of the Lord who had strengthened her in those early days.

After teaching for six years in Zimbabwe and Zambia, the Wilkenses returned home to the United States. But it wasn't long before Africa was calling again. This time it was to serve in a beautiful, peaceful country where there hadn't been a major war in many years. "You looked at the map, and it was this tiny little country in the center of the continent. Its elevation was such that even though it was near the equator, the weather was gorgeous." It seemed like an ideal place for the Wilkens family, who now had three children ranging in age from almost two to six.

Their first six months in this new country were idyllic. Carl took up his responsibilities as the director of the Adventist Development and Relief Agency (ADRA). "We traveled around this mountainous country, the Land of a Thousand Hills," he told me. "I mean, it's so gorgeous the people there have this traditional belief that God sleeps in Rwanda. He goes about the rest of the world and does His work, but at nighttime He comes home to this little country in the center of Africa. Before the genocide, nobody knew much about Rwanda, except maybe about the gorillas. Perhaps they had seen that old movie *Gorillas in the Mist* about Dian Fossey. But that's all they knew about this tiny little country about a hundred miles by a hundred miles on the bellybutton of Africa. Sadly, today it's known for genocide. But when we went there, it was like a really ideal posting."

But that country now lives in the world's memory as the location of the most rapid and deadly genocide of the twentieth century. In the one hundred days from April 7 through July 17, 1994, it is conservatively estimated that eight hundred thousand Rwandans—approximately 10 percent of the nation's population—were murdered by their fellow countrymen.

On April 6, 1994, two surface-to-air missiles were fired at a small jet as it came in for a landing at Kigali International Airport in Rwanda's capital city. Aboard the jet were the presidents of Rwanda and neighboring Burundi, along with several cabinet members from the Rwandan government. At least one of the missiles struck the plane, and it crashed, killing all aboard.

While some people thought the missile attack was the act of rebels, or just a random act, Carl believes it was part of a well-planned coup. "Within forty-five minutes, they started putting up roadblocks around the city," he told me. "Asking people for their ID cards, because your ID card was going to be the ticket to whether you lived or whether you died; whether you were part of the Hutu majority, or whether you were part of the Tutsi minority."

Based on his experiences in the country during the three years leading up to that day, Carl is convinced that the ensuing events were carefully planned by a group of people who did not want to relinquish or share political power. Tensions had been growing for several months, and there had been sporadic fighting and bombing in the city. "They had been organizing and planning, training people, broadcasting hate messages on the radio; all kinds of preparation went into it. There's nothing spontaneous about a genocide," he says.

But overall, up to that time, Carl believed that things were on the uptick in Rwanda. In fact, after a period of civil war, things seemed to be settling down enough in early 1994, that Carl had invited his father to come to the country to help oversee the finances of a project of rebuilding clinics that had been damaged during the strife.

Carl and his father were working in downtown Kigali on April 6 when the power went out in that part of the city, and they decided to return home. After dinner, about eight o'clock that night, they heard a loud explosion. They didn't think a lot about it at the moment, but Carl's dad did remark that it was louder than the average grenade explosion. Grenade explosions and gunfire were part of everyday life in the city. But this time Carl wondered out loud whether rebel troops might have blown up an ammunition dump or something.

Twenty minutes later, they received a phone call from a fellow missionary, informing them that the president's plane had been shot down.

From that point on, things started to change fast. The Wilkens family lived in a rented house in a suburb of Kigali, about five miles from the airport. Within an hour, they began to hear gunfire and screams in their own neighborhood. Doors were being bashed in, and people were being killed just down the street from them. The next day, they saw armed men walking down the street carrying furniture they had looted from neighbors' houses after killing the neighbors.

"The second night, Thursday night, they came to our gate," Carl told me. "But we didn't know about it until the next morning. Our neighbors came and stood up for us. It's incredible when you look into the faces of these ladies— grandmothers, aunts. You think, *What would get me to come out of my house if there were riots going on in the streets, and there was gunfire, and I'm trying to keep the kids away from the window and things like that? What would get me to come out of my house and stand in front of the gate of a foreigner, and say, 'No, you can't come in'?* I mean, these are guys with machetes, with clubs studded with spikes. They've got adrenaline racing through them following the horrible things they've been doing to others. What are you going to say to them that will actually stop them?"

In talking with his neighbors later, Carl learned that they had simply told the killers that there were nice foreigners that lived in this house, that they had done acts of kindness in the community, and that their children played with the neighbor-hood children. "I've come to understand their actions: they rehumanized Teresa and myself, our kids. At that moment, that dark night there, before they came in—and they never did come into our house—they somehow managed through stories to rehumanize our family, and the killers moved on."

The concepts of dehumanizing and rehumanizing people have become very important to Carl and Teresa through the years. In fact, today they travel around the country trying to help young people understand that hateful rhetoric, teasing, and bullying de-humanize people and can lead to tragic consequences.

By Friday, it was plain that no one who stayed in Rwanda would be safe for long. Carl learned that the entire diplomatic staff of the American embassy, including the ambassador, was preparing for evacuation. Because the airport had become part of a battle zone, the evacuation would be taking place by road, going to neighboring Burundi.

Now Carl and Teresa had to decide what to do. The embassy was advising all Americans to leave the country immediately. Anyone who wanted to stay would have to sign a paper stating that they had turned down the chance to be evacuated along with the embassy staff.

It was clear that Carl's father, mother, Teresa, and the children needed to get out of the country. But what would Carl do? "I couldn't see my way clear, saying to my Rwandan friends and colleagues, 'Look, I've got this passport, and I'm leaving. I'll pray for you.'

"It's not like I don't believe in prayer. It's like God said, 'Wait!' If He would be with them, why wouldn't He be with me?"

And then there was Anitha, the young woman who had lived with and worked for their family, taking care of their children. And there was the night watchman. Their ID cards listed them as Tutsi. Turning them out onto the street would be a death sentence.

With a heavy heart, Carl bade farewell to his family as they loaded into a little homemade camper truck and headed to the American ambassador's home to join the last convoy out of Rwanda.

Having lived through tumultuous times before, they felt sure that the separation wouldn't last long. Carl figured he'd be able to go visit his family in Burundi within a couple of weeks, and in three weeks, they would be able to move back to Rwanda, and life would go on as before.

"But in reality, it was three weeks before I even left the house!" Carl revealed.

During those three weeks, curfews were supposedly enforced all over the city. But it didn't stop the killing. The only people out on the streets most of the time were the killers. Carl brought several other people, including a pastor's family, into the house for protection. And for those three weeks, they survived by collecting rainwater off the roof and bartering through the fence with neighbors, and even with looters who were going about town selling stolen food and toilet paper.

Fortunately, Carl had a shortwave radio in the house, and he was able to communicate with Teresa every day. In Burundi, she was able to use a radio at the American embassy. Later, when she and the children were evacuated to Nairobi, Kenya, friends who worked with the Doctors Without Borders organization loaned her a radio that she could use at home so the children could join her in talking to their daddy.

"One particular conversation I remember from that time," Teresa said, "was our daughter telling Carl on the radio—complaining—because her little brother had thrown a rock at her and her friends. Carl's response was, 'I guess Shaun needs his daddy, doesn't he?' And our daughter, Mindy, said after a moment, 'Not as much as those orphans need you, Daddy.' "

"Wow!" was all I could say in response to that. Carl and Teresa's little girl was learning at that early age the importance and meaning of service to others.

By this time Carl was able to get out of the house and move about the city, looking for opportunities to help. It was still very dangerous—people were still being killed by the thousands every day, and there were still roadblocks everywhere. United Nations troops found it almost impossible to get around, and the Red Cross had quit sending people out because too many of their workers had been murdered while on errands of mercy.

Carl told me that the only way to survive and be able to do any good in a situation like that is through building relationships.

But what do you do when the only people who can make it possible for you to help those in need are the very people at the center of the heinous crimes going on around you?

Carl somehow knew what to do. He made contact with the army colonel who had control of the troops and civilian militias in the city and asked how he as the director of ADRA could be of help. One of the colonel's associates told him about two orphanages that needed supplies.

On his first visit to one of the orphanages, Carl saw freshly dug graves. Children were dying of starvation and of dysentery. He knew he needed to get clean water, food, and medicines to them as soon as possible. So he began going into the street markets, inquiring of vendors where they were getting their supplies. Then he would go to the suppliers—usually a partnership between a soldier and a civilian—and purchase, from their stolen loot, quantities of the needed items.

But he knew that if he loaded up his car with supplies and delivered them all at once to the orphanage, people would take note. As soon as he left, there would be a raid, and everything he had delivered would be stolen.

So, rather than let that happen, he went back to the colonel and persuaded him to make room in a closet at the headquarters building. From there Carl could operate safely, distributing supplies in small enough quantities that it didn't attract the attention of looters.

All the while though, killing was going on in the city, and one of the orphanages was located in one of the most dangerous parts of town. Working through intermediaries, in order to avoid being labeled as a Tutsi lover, Carl managed to get the orphans moved to a safer place.

But then the challenge remained: how to get their bedding and supplies moved?

That's when Carl found himself working side by side with murderers.

"You could never imagine these guys we thought were going to murder us three days earlier, were now helping us load the truck," he said.

From working with all kinds of people through this horrific time, Carl developed a deep understanding of the potential for both good and evil that lies hidden in each of our hearts. In the course of a day, some of these people would be both taking lives and saving lives. Average, ordinary people who had lived in peace with one another for generations suddenly could be transformed into enraged killers; but, at the same time, others would risk their lives to save perfect strangers. And people who were out killing on the streets might be hiding friends at home to keep them safe.

That's why Carl and Teresa have dedicated their lives these

days to helping young people learn how to make the right choices. Since 2004 they've been traveling all over the country, speaking to high school, university, and civic groups about their experience in Rwanda and trying to help people see the danger inherent in what they call "us and them thinking" that creates enmity against people we perceive as being different from us. They've founded an educational and development organization called World Outside My Shoes, whose goal is to help people understand each other better by getting acquainted and coming to understand what life is like for people who live under different circumstances—who walk in different moccasins. (Maybe you've heard the old adage: Never criticize a man till you've walked a mile in his moccasins.)

Recently at one school, a young woman asked Carl why he bothers going around speaking to students. Why not spend his time talking to people who have more money and influence?

Carl reminded her that even high school students do have some money and influence. Then he said, "But more important than either of those is you haven't decided yet to settle for less. You haven't bought into the lie that life's that way; get used to it. The sooner you get used to it, the happier you'll be. That's a lie! Because you haven't decided to settle for less, you're not getting less."

Carl and Teresa have never been ones to settle for less. They've devoted their lives to service, and they continue serving others by pouring their lives into helping young people decide not to settle for less. I admire what they're doing, because in helping others, in living for Jesus, they're Really Living!

---

If you would like to know more about Carl and Teresa and their current work, you can learn more at http://worldoutsidemyshoes.org.

# Little Lady, Large Heart

## Bernie Irwin

Dr. Bernadine Irwin's story is the story of a lot of little things that add up to something big.

Bernie's not a very big person—physically. But what she does for some of the neediest people in her world reveals a large heart—a heart that has a huge impact on more lives than she can count.

I began the program with Bernie by talking about the kind of ministry she carries on and the type of person I would expect to be involved in such an outreach. She works with gangs, you see, in one of the rougher parts of Greater Los Angeles. And if you asked me what kind of a person ought to work in that environment, I would immediately begin picturing a great big hulk of a man, probably a weight lifter. Somebody with a deep voice and big fists who could make people sit up and listen when he spoke.

Then I brought Bernie on camera, and everybody could see that she doesn't even come up to my shoulder.

But she's the one doing gang ministry, not me.

For Bernie, this facet of her ministry began with a girl named Jessica.

Bernie has been involved in working with young people for many years. But it was what happened to Jessica that moved her from a more general involvement into becoming the founder of a program designed specifically to help disadvantaged kids break free of gang environments and gang mentalities so that they have bet-

ter chances of making something good out of their lives.

Jessica Salazar was a beautiful young woman whose dreams were an inspiration to Bernie, who met her while leading groups at the San Bernardino County Youth Justice Center. Troubled young people and those on parole for crimes can continue their high school educations there.

"As I got acquainted with Jessica and caught a glimpse of the incredible potential she had, and had the privilege of hearing from her—her dream of growing up and getting an education and making a difference with other kids in gangs—I just was inspired," Bernie told me.

Unfortunately, Jessica's dreams of helping kids to get out of gangs came to a crashing halt in February 2000, just weeks after her fourteenth birthday, when she was kidnapped and murdered by alleged gang members.

Dr. Irwin and several other Loma Linda University staff members attended a memorial service for Jessica; and something Bernie learned when she went to the cemetery sank deep down into her heart and made her realize she needed to try to do something to improve the lives—and the chances to live—for young people like Jessica.

"We learned that several of Jessica's classmates couldn't go to the graveside service," she told me.

"Why not?" I asked.

"Because of her death being gang related, they would be at risk of being gunned down!"

The tragedy of Jessica's untimely death, along with the second tragedy of young people having to live in fear for their very lives if they were to stray into the wrong geographical territory, even to the cemetery where their friend was being buried, was too much for Bernie to take. It made her want to stand up and do something about it.

What she did first was write the book *For the Love of Jessica,* which tells the stories of young people's lives that have been transformed through the programs she offered at the Youth Justice Center.

But she wanted to do something more. "Jesus kindled a passion in my heart, an irrepressible love for these kids," Bernie told me. "Before, when I would see gang kids, I would be afraid. But now, I recognize what a privilege it is to get to know them and make a difference in their lives."

Bernie was determined to find new ways to bring change to the troubled kids, and God soon opened a door for her.

Right after the book *For the Love of Jessica* came out, a gentleman approached Bernie. He said that he'd had a lot of dreams in his life, and that many of them had focused around making money. A lot of those dreams had come true. In fact, the company he was the head of had made fourteen billion dollars in profits the previous year.

"I was touched by Jessica's story," the man told Bernie. "Is there any way that you and I could partner to make a difference?"

Bernie was quick to respond, "Let's sit down and dream together what that might look like!"

The dream that took shape was a program called Operation Jessica, which brings troubled youth together with Loma Linda University students who serve as mentors to try to help the youth find new focuses for their lives.

This is done with four-day retreats held in a wilderness setting. The troubled youths who are to participate are selected on the basis of how well they are doing in their group-home setting. They aren't told much about what they're getting involved in until they're already a part of it. They just get an invitation to go away to a youth camp in the mountains for four days.

Aikeem Roberts, one of the participants, came on the *Really Living* set and described what the experience had been like. At the time he was a high school student who had lived almost his entire life in a succession of foster homes and group homes. His mother and father split up when he was just six months old; he's never even met his father and has seen his mother only a few times in his life.

For a time, he was kept in the same home with an older brother, but counselors feared that the brother was having a bad influence on him, so they separated the siblings. Things went from bad to worse for Aikeem after that. Because he missed his brother, he started getting into more trouble, and his grades suffered.

After a time, his behavior must have improved some because he told me that he was invited to go on the Operation

Jessica retreat based on how well he was doing in his group home. He didn't know much about what to expect; he was just told to be sure to bring gloves, a hat, and a warm sweater because they were going to the mountains.

When the day of the retreat came, Aikeem and other young people from group and foster homes loaded into a bus with an equal number of mentors from Loma Linda University, along with other staff members, for the ride to the mountains.

I asked him what it was like once they got to the camp.

"It was pretty fun," he said. "We had a lot of new challenges that we had to face, like the rope climbing. We had to climb real, real high, and jump off at the end. But you have to go a distance across, about thirty feet up. On one of them, you're actually on the rope by yourself—nobody's holding you, nobody can make sure you don't fall, but only a rope—you have to trust the rope to save your life. It feels like you're going to die. But you don't. It's pretty scary, though. You're just shaking."

Of course, he also told me about lots of fun activities, such as riding go-karts and mountain bikes. Then I asked him if there was anything that happened there that changed his life.

A look of peace and joy came over his face, as he recalled, "Waking up every morning, meeting in the Ponderosa Room, where we'd have a prayer before breakfast." He smiled a little sheepishly as he confessed that "breakfast is no meat, so people do get kind of discouraged to go, but it's vegetarian food, it's pretty good."

After breakfast, the participants and mentors split up into groups for various activities.

Dr. Bernie explained to me how the program runs and

what they try to accomplish. "Our primary goal is spiritual transformation of gang kids," she told me. They take the kids out in nature in order to help get them out of the negative environment they've grown up in and to give them time to connect with a mentor, time to gain a new perspective on life, and time to develop some better strategies for dealing with their world.

To this end, staff members lead participants through five group sessions. The first looks at the victims and survivors. All of the participants have been victims in some way, and through dramas, skits, and music, they are helped to come to terms with what has happened. In a moving ceremony at the end of the first session, candles are passed out to each of the troubled youths. The candles are lit, and the group gathers in the center of a darkened room. Then they are told that if they have been the victims of abuse, or if they have friends or family members who have been victims, they should blow out the candle. Candles start going out immediately. When the leader says that those who have known someone who was murdered should blow out their candles, more lights go out.

At the end of this exercise, the room is totally dark. "We tell them," Bernie said, "that we know that they have had a lot of darkness in the past, but that a part of Operation Jessica is bringing the light back into lives."

I can only imagine how moving an experience that must be as candle after candle is blown out, but then the kids hear of ways that they can have new light in their lives, find new reasons to hope, and make plans for a better future.

The second group session is a presentation about unhealthy coping—behaviors the young people have used to try to get by in life—"to live within the shells they've had to build around themselves," as Bernie puts it. These might include unhealthy sex, drugs, violence, or involvement in gangs.

In a third session, the topic is healing of wounds. The focus this time is very spiritual. Jesus Christ is presented to the young people as the Son of God who came to earth to take our wounds upon Himself. During the session, the participants are given a sheet of paper to write about the wounds that they have suffered in life. At the end of the session, they place that sheet of paper in an envelope and then hang the envelope on a cross. Many tears are shed as the participants come to realize that they have a Savior who came to bear their wounds and their pain. Later that evening, at a campfire meeting, they take the envelopes down off the cross and incinerate them.

After dealing with all of those negative things, the fourth session at the Operation Jessica retreat turns to the positive. In a presentation on personal possibilities, the participants are encouraged to look at their lives, focusing on the positive dreams they have. They hear stories of other individuals who have come out of difficult circumstances and have lived out their dreams.

In the fifth and final session, the Operation Jessica pastor shares his personal experience of coming out of years of cocaine use, but by the grace of God, experiencing healing and recovery. The pastor goes to each of the teenagers individually, hands him or her a key, and talks to that individual about the dreams that he understands the teenager has. When he hands them the keys, "you'd think he was handing them a million dollars," Bernie told me.

These four-day retreats have proved to be transformational in the lives of many young people, including Aikeem. I'll tell you in a moment what he shared with me about how his life was changed. But before we get to that, I want to tell you about another group of young people.

Operation Jessica couldn't be successful without the dedicated service of this other group, the mentors, who are drawn from the student body of Loma Linda University. Most of them are nursing students, but students from other disciplines are welcome to apply as well.

Dr. Bernie brought one of these mentors with her—a young lady named Myrna—and I asked Myrna what it meant to her to be a mentor.

"It's a real privilege to be a mentor," Myrna said. "It was an awesome experience. It was just another way of sharing God's love. We had four days with the teens. The first day we met them was on the bus, when we picked them up. We didn't know them, but through the course of the week, we got to form this bond that's just amazing.

"You're up in the mountains, you don't know what to expect when you go into this program, but I got to experience another confirmation of how great God's love is for anyone—no matter how deep the wound is, how ugly their past was, God can go in there and heal and work His miracles, no matter what stage you are in your life."

After talking with Myrna, I began to suspect that the Operation Jessica program isn't just about helping disadvantaged teens. It's also about helping the university students who are preparing for careers in medicine. Another of my guests on this program confirmed my suspicions.

Dr. Marti Baum is a pediatrician who is also a member of the faculty of Loma Linda University. She joined us to talk about why she wants her students to be involved in programs like Operation Jessica. "We have so many miracle treatments in medicine now," she said. "In the hospital, medical residents are getting training in how to make a difference, how to be in charge, and actually save patients. But we are not doing such a good job on the street.

"What we are trying to do is to empower these residents to look beyond the place where it's easy to be successful—which is in the hospital—and to look for the harder job, which is working with the kids on the street. Before they come into the ICU (intensive care unit) and they've been gunned down, or before they come into the emergency room and they've been stabbed, or before they become homeless."

The program is working on that side as well. Dr. Baum told me the story of a timid young resident who had her eyes opened to a whole new world of possibilities for service. This young woman had been very sheltered throughout her life. She volunteered for Operation Jessica, and then found herself on a bus with a bunch of big guys who looked very scary to her. "She came out of the bus with eyes as big as saucers," Dr. Baum said. "She just looked at me, and she goes, 'Dr. Marti, I don't know if I can do this.' And I said, 'No, you'll be able to find the strength.'

"She found herself climbing trees, she found herself becoming involved and very connected with her mentee. On the very final day, she was in tears as she told her story of how this had been the biggest stretch she had ever made, and that God was so important to her in her own life, and it was very special to her to be able to share this with another kid who, previously, she would have crossed the street to avoid."

In conclusion, the young mentor told the group that her life had been transformed, and that now she had a new mission for her life—working with teens!

So, lives are being transformed through Operation Jessica. For his part, Aikeem told me that he has a whole new set of goals for his life since attending the retreat. He may go into the military or perhaps the job corps. After that he plans to attend college and get a degree in computer graphic design. He has already graduated from high school, and he's living on his own now. Looking at him, seeing the confidence in his expression, the gentleness with which he spoke, and the love he expressed to those who had helped him, I knew that here was a young man whose life had genuinely been transformed and that we can expect great things for him.

My hat is off to Dr. Bernie Irwin, Dr. Marti Baum, to Myrna, to Aikeem, and to all of the faculty, students, and teenagers involved in Operation Jessica. These people are Really Living! And they are helping countless others begin to really live as well.

# Turning Churches Into Centers of Compassion

## Oscar and Eugenia Giordano

I'm convinced that the Lord must have certain special people on this planet whom He seeks out and calls to very special ministries, and I'm also convinced that Oscar and Eugenia Giordano are two of those people. They are having a fantastic impact for the Lord on a continent that is not their home—at least it wasn't their home in the beginning. In fact, the place they live and serve now is the third continent that they have called home.

When I spoke with the doctors Giordano—both Oscar and Eugenia are physicians—they told me that a few years ago they were Christians, but not committed Christians. Having been raised in believing homes, they had a general sense of what Christianity was, but it wasn't the most important thing in their lives.

Both of them were born in Argentina, and that is where they met. With a smile, they described a special holiday in Argentina celebrated on September 21—the first day of spring in the Southern Hemisphere. I'm not sure what all was going on that day, but they told me it is a special day for students, and that the two of them were in the park, and that is where they met.

Sometime later, Eugenia's family moved to the United States. But there must have been something really special about that fellow she met in the park that day, because it wasn't long until she found her way back to Argentina, where the two of them were married.

Both attended medical school in their home country and then moved to the United States, planning to go on for further training. But before they could fulfill that plan, something else happened, something that would change their walk with the Lord for the rest of their lives.

"We knew about God, but something was missing," Oscar told me. "There was an emptiness that we needed to fill. And this is the wonderful thing that happened soon after we arrived in the States."

Eugenia picked up the story: "We were living in Oceanside, in the San Diego area, and many denominations were coming to our door, and we were listening to all of them, but something was not right. Oscar had an idea—something was impressing him."

"God impressed me," Oscar continued, "that the church we were looking for had to be one hundred percent Bible based. I don't know where this came from, but it was strongly impressed in my mind, so I shared it with Eugenia, and we both decided to look for a church that was one hundred percent Bible based."

The little family knelt together and asked the Lord to show them where to go. A few days later, their young daughter lost her purse in a park near their home. She was very distraught about it, so the next morning as soon as the sun was up, Oscar took her to the park to look for it. There was no one else there except the gardener, so they asked him if he had seen a purse. To the great relief of the little girl, the gardener had the purse and gladly gave it to them.

Unbeknownst to them, this was the beginning of the answer to their prayer for guidance. The gardener became their friend and came by to visit from time to time. Then one day, he said to Oscar, "How is your spiritual life?"

That opened the door to some important discussions of religion, and it wasn't long before the gardener had invited them to attend his church. But there was something odd about this church—he invited them to come on Saturday! But because he was a good friend and they had learned to trust him, they decided to give it a try.

"When we arrived to that little church in Vista, California, we felt so good," they told me. "We felt welcomed. You know, these people—most of them from Mexico—they were so loving that from the first day we felt loved by them. So that was the beginning of us going to the Seventh-day Adventist Church, and since then we never fail to go."

Oscar spoke with wonder of something that he observed that first day in church. "I remember in that first time we visited that church, a person that prayed at the end of the main service touched my heart. I told Eugenia, 'I wish that one day, with all that I have studied, and all the books I have read, that I can pronounce those words.' "

The two doctors were clearly deeply impressed by the humble spirituality they witnessed in that little church, and I can't help but think that in that experience God was preparing them for the ministry He had selected them for—a ministry that would touch the lives of many humble people on a distant continent, back in the hemisphere of their birth.

Oscar and Eugenia and their four children soon became very active in the church, and they developed a burning desire to lead other people to the Lord. At La Sierra University, Oscar began taking classes in theology, taught by a visiting professor from Andrews University. He began to feel more and more deeply that he wanted to become a pastor, so he spoke to the professor.

"Why do you want to become a pastor?" the professor asked.

"Because I want to win souls for Jesus."

"Oscar, you are a physician. God can use you to win souls for Christ."

"How?"

The professor quoted Isaiah 30:21. "And thine ears shall hear a word behind thee, saying, This is the way, walk ye in it, when ye turn to the right hand, and when ye turn to the left" (KJV).

"How am I going to hear that Voice?" Oscar asked.

"Pray about it, and you will see," the professor said.

At first, that didn't seem like a very satisfactory answer. How were they supposed to hear a Voice? God had never spoken to them from the skies in the past. Why should they expect something like that to happen now?

Eugenia picked up the story from there: "What happened is that the following week—we had never thought about going to anywhere—but the following week three different persons talked to us, and said, 'Hey, what are you doing here? I thought you were in Africa!' "

At the end of the week, a friend invited them to attend a meeting where a woman who had been serving as a missionary shared her experiences from the mission field.

They were hearing voices, all right, maybe not voices from the sky, but they were clearly being impressed that perhaps God had a place for them in mission work. And so this family that had already left their home country and adopted a new country put in an application to serve as missionaries somewhere else.

Nothing happened right away, but a year later, they received a call from the world headquarters of the Seventh-day Adventist Church, inviting them to go as missionaries to Rwanda, Africa. Because it seemed like an answer to prayer, they jumped at the chance. As they read about Rwanda, they were pleased to learn that it was one of the most peaceful countries in Africa, a beautiful place often referred to as the Switzerland of Africa.

"We had three and one half years of peace," Oscar told me. During those years, Oscar served as the only surgeon in a 104-bed hospital as well as serving as the administrator of the hospital. Eugenia served with one other clinician, meeting the needs of eighty or more outpatients per day, plus the needs of those occupying the 104 beds.

I probably don't need to remind you that in April of 1994, a horrible civil war broke out in Rwanda between the Hutu and Tutsi tribes.

The war broke out on a Wednesday.

Two days earlier, Oscar had driven the six and a half hours from their mission hospital to the capital city, Kigali, taking their oldest daughter to the airport so she could fly to Nairobi, Kenya, for school.

The outbreak of war found Oscar still in Kigali, while Eugenia and their three other children were at the mission hospital. Oscar went frantically from agency to agency, contacting the United Nations and others groups, trying to find help to get back to the hospital, but nobody could help him. Finally, he realized he would have to make the trip on his own.

On his own, *with an angel escort,* that is. "Thanks to God, I made it," he says. "That was a miracle, because the war was on, and I had to go through all those villages, but the Lord protected me in a special way. I think I did the trip faster than ever—it was not an easy trip in the mountains with roads that are not good, and the circumstances, but the Lord helped me. I arrived at night, and when I saw the lights in the windows of our house—all this, you know, you do it praying constantly."

By this time bands of vigilantes were roaming throughout the country, killing and wreaking havoc wherever they went. Streams of people with serious injuries and wounds were flowing into the hospital, and the two doctors set about doing what they could to help. But the next day, the radio broadcast the news that all expatriates were being expelled from the country. They had until eight o'clock the following night to find their way out of Uganda!

What could they do? They talked with their staff members, who urged them to leave. They were the only expatriates in the area, and they would surely be the targets of any violence that might come. So, with heavy hearts, they packed what they could into their car, and made what medicines and food they had available to the people in the hospital, then headed south toward the border with Zaire.

"It was a long trip, and very painful," Oscar told me.

You might expect that after a harrowing experience like that, the family would want to return to their home country. But not the Giordanos. They were willing to stay in Africa, and soon they were assigned to help reorganize the health work of the church in Burundi, the nation just south of Rwanda. But as the war continued in Rwanda, huge refugee camps formed on the borders, and Oscar was asked to help out in one of those camps. The rest of the family was given a place to stay in Burundi, but soon even that would not be available.

Because of tensions and threats, church leaders told Eugenia and the children that they needed to move to Kenya, which left Dr. Oscar alone, working in the refugee camp. This went on for about eleven months, with only occasional visits to his family in Kenya.

Finally, though, the difficult situation in the refugee camp began taking its toll on him, and his own health began to suffer. So it was decided that the family should take a temporary assignment on the island of Madagascar, off the east coast of Africa.

When I heard about all the troubles, difficulties, and health problems they had encountered in their work, I asked Oscar and Eugenia about the leading of the Lord in their lives. "We started out talking about putting your hand in the hand of God," I said. "Was it in God's hand there?"

Oscar and Eugenia's way of answering me was to tell me a story about one of their daughters. When they left Burundi, they took a trip through Rwanda, which by then was peaceful once again. When they arrived at their old home on the hospital compound, they could see that everything had been looted. Nothing remained of the things they had left behind. The hospital, too, was in ruins. But the part of that experience that has stuck with them happened several months later, when Eugenia saw a paper her third daughter had written for school.

The girl had been just twelve years old when they visited their former home in Rwanda and found it in ruins. But in her school paper, she wrote, "The Lord has been leading in our lives. When I saw our house, I had peace in my heart instead of having bad feelings. So I knew that the Lord was giving me that peace."

That made a deep impression on me; when I saw that out of all the trials they had gone through, the most important thing those missionary parents remembered was that the bad things that had happened had taught their daughter to trust more in God!

The Giordanos were supposed to work in Madagascar for only three months, but they ended up staying there for nearly nine years. "And let me tell you," Eugenia said, "those nine years were the highlight of our lives. The Lord was so good! Everything was blessed! Everything prospered! Everything was wonderful!"

The two doctors, working together, were able to get the hospital staffed with well-trained workers and to organize a very effective health outreach.

But then, just when it seemed that they ought to finally be able to relax and enjoy the fruit of their hard work, guess what? Another call came from church headquarters.

This time they were being asked to completely change

their line of work. Church administrators wanted them to stop working as physicians and begin working in the field of public health. Specifically, they were being requested to set up an office for HIV and AIDS ministry in Africa.

They knew this was something that was much needed on that continent, because they had witnessed the ravages of the disease in Rwanda. In fact, in the region where their hospital was located, 32 percent of the population was known to be HIV-positive! That means approximately a third of the population was infected with the HIV virus, which eventually leads to AIDS, as the virus compromises people's immune systems. Infection levels vary from region to region, but Oscar told me that the disease is so widespread that there is not one family in all of Africa that has not been touched in some way by this modern-day plague.

Now they were being called upon to develop and coordinate a program to help the Seventh-day Adventist churches in Africa do something to stop the spread of the disease. "It's a huge challenge, Don," Oscar told me, "especially considering that we have about sixteen thousand churches and congregations, with five million members, and we need to reach them and provide understanding of the epidemic, methods of prevention, and then supportive care for the ones who are already affected—without forgetting the communities around our churches."

What could they possibly do to alleviate such a pervasive problem? It was no surprise to me when they told me that the first part of their solution was to pray about it. At first it seemed to them that it would take millions of dollars to institute any sort of effective program. But the more they prayed and studied their Bibles, the more they began to think, rather, of what Jesus would do.

As they did this, the words of Jesus found in Matthew 25:35, 36, began to take on new meaning. They began to paraphrase it this way: "I was hungry, and you gave Me something to eat. I was thirsty, and you gave Me something to drink. I was sick with AIDS, and you took care of Me. I was naked, and you clothed Me. I was a stranger, an orphan, and you invited Me in. I was in prison, and you visited Me."

As they meditated and prayed over the ministry and methods of Jesus, a new vision of how to minister to the continent of Africa began to take shape in their minds. Why couldn't they help people in the same way that Jesus did? Why couldn't each church begin to meet the needs of the community, serving in the way that Jesus had done—reaching out and touching the people, bringing healing and teaching?

They knew that Jesus' way of ministry included meeting people's felt needs, so they took surveys in various countries, asking the people what was most needed there. Always the first need to come up on the list was food. They found that a lot of training and teaching had already been done—the people had heard plenty of talk about how to prevent the spread of AIDS—but they still needed food. People were getting treatments for AIDS, but because their nutrition was so poor, they weren't regaining their strength.

Oscar and Eugenia realized that there was no way that the church could supply food to all the millions of starving people, but that there was something better they could do. They could teach people how to raise their own food in more effective ways; they could help them get good seeds, chickens, goats, even honeybees that would give them the potential to raise more food than their family needed, and even bring in some income. So, that's what they did.

"The plan is to empower and equip our churches and our

church members to deal with the epidemic," Oscar told me. "It is a comprehensive program that includes prevention, care, and support, but also includes income generation as part of the support."

Another area of desperate need that their studies quickly revealed focused on the grandmothers in Africa. Nobody knew why, but a lot of the older women—far past childbearing age—were testing as HIV-positive. As they looked more closely at the problem, they discovered that these women had been neglected in AIDS-related education. Nobody thought that they were at risk.

But what was actually happening was that these women were finding themselves on the front lines in dealing with the epidemic, because their children were becoming infected and dying. The old women would tend to their children until they died, and then they would take on responsibility for their grandchildren. But they had not been given any education about how to protect themselves from infection. Anybody who has raised small children knows that the caretakers will, at some time, be exposed to blood. Without proper precautions, the grandmothers were becoming infected by their children or their grandchildren.

So Oscar and Eugenia decided to create a ministry focused on grandmothers, empowering them with education so that they would know how to protect themselves when they handled blood.

What they did was to start grandmothers' clubs.

"These grandmothers, you cannot imagine—they are so powerful!" Eugenia says. "They can do food gardens, they can do sewing, they can work in the villages, they can do so many things!"

The grandmothers' clubs are just one part of a comprehensive program that is turning churches throughout Africa into support groups and support centers for the community.

The support groups and support centers reach out to the community in many different ways, not just with HIV and AIDS support. If a house burns down in the village, church members are there to help the displaced family. If someone has cancer, the church will help them as well.

"We all need support in our lives," Oscar reminded me. "So, we want to empower our churches to have these support groups to help in any circumstance within the church and outside the church."

Eugenia joined in, sharing her dream. "Can you imagine if each of our churches would have a support group—a group of people that are there that meet every week to help themselves and to help the surrounding community? Our church would be known as a church of compassion."

"We are talking about a ministry of compassion here," Oscar added.

A ministry of compassion, indeed. It's more than an abstract concept for Oscar and Eugenia Giordano. It seems to flow from their very pores. I asked Eugenia, "Are you afraid of getting AIDS?"

"No."

I wondered if she felt like it couldn't happen to her, but she continued, "It can happen to anybody. But I am not afraid."

Not afraid, not afraid to show compassion, not afraid to reach out and touch those in the deepest need—that sounds like Jesus to me. It sounds like Really Living.

# From Daughter of Communism to Child of God

## Rebekah Liu

Rebekah Liu and her family know for sure that you can't start Really Living until you meet Jesus. They tried a lot of other things on their way to receiving the gospel, but none of them were satisfying.

Today, Rebekah and her family proclaim the good news about Jesus in a nation whose historical experience with Christian peoples led its government to turn against Christianity. And they are helping their fellow citizens learn that the religion that their ancestors rejected was not the real thing. They are teaching thousands how to find the real Christianity and to give their lives to the real Jesus. Their story—particularly Rebekah's mother's story—is an amazing testimony to the power of God to change lives.

By all rights you would expect Rebekah to be a devoted, atheistic Communist. Born in China to a "daughter of Communism," she was thoroughly indoctrinated in Communist ideals. She grew up thinking of Chairman Mao Zedong as the savior for her people, and she knew that Christianity was the religion of the foreign imperialists who had used military force to impose unfair treaties on China, forcing the people to import and use opium.

Rebekah told me some things about the history of religion in

China that surprised me. She explained that Chinese people are pragmatic about spiritual things. Historically, they've followed the ethical teachings of Confucianism, along with the principles of Buddhism and Taoism, with a healthy measure of Chinese traditions added into the mix. Basically, she said, whatever works for them, that's what they do.

As for Christianity in China, it has a dark history, which Rebekah reviewed briefly for me. Back in the 1840s, Great Britain and China went to war over something that seems astonishing to us today. British traders were exporting opium from India to China, and were forcing the Chinese to accept the drug against their own government's wishes. The drug was wreaking havoc on the lives of many Chinese people, turning once-productive citizens into helpless addicts.

When the Chinese attempted to stop the opium trade, Britain declared war. And when the British emerged victorious, they forced China to submit to what came to be known as the "unequal treaties." These treaties forced China to keep importing British opium against its will.

The thing that gave Christianity a bad name in China was that the same treaties that gave British traders the right to sell opium there also made demands concerning religion.

That's right, the same unjust treaties that forced the Chinese to accept narcotics also imposed religion—specifically the Christian religion—on China. The treaties included a stipulation that along with the opium the Chinese had to allow Christian missionaries!

Wow! I had never thought about that from a Chinese perspective before, but when Rebekah explained it to me, I could see why many Chinese people didn't associate Christianity with a loving Savior, but instead with violent foreign domination.

The repressive attitude of Western countries (viewed as representatives of Christianity by the Chinese) continued right up to and beyond the Boxer Rebellion at the beginning of the twentieth century.

In the early years of that century, Chinese people began to look for ways to advance their nation and free it from foreign oppression. Students who traveled to Russia and France came back with glowing reports about the sort of equality that Communism promised; and in 1921, some of them founded the Chinese Communist Party, which gave rise to the Chinese Red Army.

A few years later, a group of Chinese Red Army soldiers arrived in the city where Rebekah's grandparents lived. Her grandfather and his brothers were all wealthy landowners, but several of them became so dedicated to Communist ideas that they gave away their land and allowed the army to divide it up among the local peasants. Her grandfather and three of his brothers then joined the army.

The Chinese Red Army emerged victorious in 1949, but of the four brothers who had marched away, only Rebekah's grandfather returned home. His three brothers had died in the fighting, giving their lives for the cause.

Because of his service, Rebekah's grandfather was regarded as a hero of the revolution, and he was appointed a judge in his city. He continued to be a strong believer in Communism, even sentencing his older brother to death for opposing the Communist government! But the hard life he had lived as a soldier, and his hard work after the revolution, took its toll. He died before his fiftieth birthday, when Rebekah's mother was just ten years old.

Because of her father's great sacrifices for the Communist cause, Rebekah's mother was given a certificate declaring that she was a martyr's daughter. This entitled her to support from the government right up to the time when she went to college. She was proud of the certificate, and extremely proud to be called a daughter of Communism.

Rebekah's mother studied Chinese literature in college, graduating in 1965. Then in 1966, the Cultural Revolution began. This was a time of great turmoil throughout China, when anything related to past culture was criticized. It continued until Chairman Mao's death in 1976. To Rebekah's family it represented the first crack in the Communist armor. Prior to the Cultural Revolution, they had thought of Communism as a panacea that would solve all of the nation's problems. But now they could see many of the system's shortcomings.

Rebekah's own upbringing taught her to have great respect for Chairman Mao as the savior of her people—in a very literal sense. As a little child, she was afraid of death, she told me. "But I thought Chairman Mao could save me. So whenever I saw that someone had died, I asked, 'Why didn't they go to Chairman Mao?' But then in 1976, Chairman Mao died. So my world just shattered. At that time I was only five. I cried a lot, and my mother cried a lot."

A few years after Mao's death, the new leader of China, Deng Xiaoping, declared that if China was to become prosperous, the nation needed to be more open economically. The principles of Communism weren't leading to prosperity, so those who were smart and knew how to make money ought to start opening businesses.

Rebekah's mother and father were both smart people. Her mother was a teacher, and her father was a chemist, so her father quit his factory job, and the family began to manufacture paint. Within a few years, they had become quite wealthy. They even had their own car, which Rebekah's mother would use to take people on tours.

Things seemed to be going well, but in later years, Rebekah's mother confessed that, even at that time she wasn't really satisfied with life. Then in 1988, Rebekah's father ran off with another woman, taking all the family's savings with him. Rebekah and her mother and brother had to survive on her mother's meager teacher's wages.

Rebekah described her mother's reaction in excellent English that still carries a fairly strong Chinese influence: "That time, my mother was very sad. The saddest part is not really poverty, because my mother knows what poverty was. The most terrible thing for her, miserable thing for her, was poverty in her mind— she had nothing to hold on to. She felt that Communism didn't work for her because of the Cultural Revolution. Then she saw that family, and earning money, could be a gospel for her, she could hold on. That didn't work. And even worse, her husband left and broke her family. So she felt, if not because of my brother and I, she would commit suicide. She was washing her face with tears all the day. So that's how she began to want to search for something more. She was desperate."

I'm glad to tell you that out of that desperation and that

search came something almost unbelievably beautiful. But, like a butterfly emerging from a chrysalis, it didn't happen without a struggle.

Looking back, Rebekah's family can see God's providence in all that had happened to them, and in what happened next.

A cousin came to visit. "Auntie, you look so sad," the cousin said. "If you don't become a Christian, you can never be happy."

The amazing part of this story is that the cousin wasn't even a Christian. But she had Christian friends, and she must have noticed that they were the happiest people she knew. One of her friends was the elder of a Christian church, and this man came to Rebekah's city to hold some meetings. The cousin urged her aunt to attend, but with her strong Communist foundation, she refused. Christianity was, after all, the religion of foreign imperialists. "My father fought to expel Christianity from this country," she said. "How can I go backward? What could I say to my father?"

The cousin persisted, however, and finally Rebekah's mother gave in and agreed to go to meet the church elder. When the elder saw her, he told her he could tell that she was not happy—which was very true. Her mother burst into tears, poured out the story of being an orphan from the time she was ten and how her husband had deserted the family.

The elder responded by telling her about the love of God, how even though all those closest to us on earth may forsake us, God loves us and will never forsake us.

Rebekah's mother rejected all of this as mere superstition. But there was something about the kindly older man that made her want to hear more. Maybe he seemed like a father figure to her. Certainly his kind, loving attitude, even when she argued with him, made it easy to keep coming back to hear more.

For ten nights she sat, listening to Christian teaching but with her guard up. She knew that even though the message was attractive, it couldn't be true. It was just Western imperialistic propaganda!

But on the way home from the last meeting, something was bothering her deep in her soul. Rebekah says that she now knows it was the Holy Spirit. But at the time, Rebekah's mother didn't even believe in God.

Still, the questions kept plaguing her mind. *If there is no God, why was the elder so persistent and loving? Did he keep telling me a lie?* Unable to fathom an answer to her questions that didn't involve believing in God, Rebekah's mother's heart began to open up to the gospel.

Rebekah saw an immediate change in her mother. She said that even after the first meeting, "her eyes were brightened."

Then, after the final meeting, her mother told her that she was going to sleep alone that night. Ever since her husband had left, she had shared her bedroom with Rebekah. Now Rebekah and the rest of the family began to be really worried. Was her mother going to become a Christian nun and renounce her family?

Fortunately, that wasn't the case. But her mother did begin attending church and studying the Bible regularly. Prior to that she had read the Book as literature, just as she had read Buddhist, Confucian, and Taoist writings. Now she began to see the Bible as the Word of God to her heart.

At the church in her city, she soon became acquainted with a man who had been a leader in the Seventh-day Adventist Church prior to the Communist revolution.

In 1979, the government allowed an organization called the Three-Self Patriotic Movement to become active once again. The three-self concept, which called for the church to be locally organized rather than controlled by outside powers, originated prior to the Communist takeover and was active under Communism prior to the Cultural Revolution but had been banned from 1966 to 1976. Church activities were driven underground into house churches in 1966.

The Three-Self Patriotic Movement united all Protestant churches into one China-based organization with no ties to denominations outside the country. The man Rebekah's mother met in church was serving as a pastor in the Three-Self church, which held worship services on Sunday. He befriended her, and eventually gave her a copy of the book *The Desire of Ages*. When she read the chapter on the Sabbath, it raised questions in her mind, so she went back to this former Adventist pastor for answers.

He told her that yes, indeed, the proper day for worship was the seventh-day Sabbath. She went to the head of the church with this information and told him she wanted to have worship services on the Sabbath at the church. But the leader told her that he wouldn't allow that.

So in 1988, taking a page from what the Christians had done during the Cultural Revolution, Rebekah's mother started a church in her home. At first there were only two members.

I haven't met Rebekah's mother, but I would like to. I'd like to look into her eyes and see the depth of fervor there—fervor that was transformed by the love of God.

Here was a woman who grew up not even believing in God, believing instead in the gospel of Communism. But when she became convicted of God's love, nothing could stop her from sharing it with others.

And when she became convicted that church ought to meet on the day that God calls holy in the Bible, she wouldn't take no for an answer.

"How many Sabbath keepers are there in your area now?" I asked Rebekah.

She told me that as of 2006 there were four hundred churches meeting on Sabbath—many of them house churches—and that there are about ten thousand members spread among those churches.

And every one of them traces their spiritual roots in some way back to Rebekah's mother's determination to be faithful to God's Ten Commandments!

I asked Rebekah what church services are like in China, and she described the church in Shanghai, which seats about fifteen hundred people. (This is, of course, no house church, but a sanctuary under the aegis of the Three-Self Patriotic Movement.)

She told me that the church is packed to overflowing every Sabbath. People have to get there early if they want to get a seat.

"What do you mean by early?" I asked.

"Six o'clock in the morning," she replied.

I was incredulous. People get to church at six o'clock in the morning?

If they aren't there by that time, they won't get in. The church doors open at 6:30 A.M. and the faithful flood in. They spend the next two hours in fellowship and prayer, then prayer meeting begins at 8:30 A.M., the worship service at 9:00 A.M., and after that they break for lunch. At 12:30 P.M. three separate meetings begin—one for those preparing for baptism, one for worker training, and another for in-depth Bible study. These meetings last until 3:00 P.M., and then people go home—nine hours after they arrived!

The church members are delighted to spend the whole day at church. To them it's a refreshing break from the work they do during the week, and many of them see it as a great educational opportunity as well.

Rebekah told me that her mother works as a pastor, she herself works as a pastor assisting her husband, and that there are many more women serving the church in China. In fact, it is conservatively estimated that approximately half of the leaders of Seventh-day Adventist house churches and larger congregations in the nation are women. It wouldn't be too far off to say that two-thirds of the leaders are women, Rebekah said.

The story of Rebekah and her mother, and the growth of Seventh-day Adventist congregations in China, is one of the most amazing stories I've heard in all the years I've been hosting the *Really Living* program.

And Rebekah's testimony of what it means to be Really Living is one of the most powerful I've heard.

"I would like to let the people in front of the TV know," she said, "that my mother's conversion story actually is a story of a searching nation. China as a nation has been searching for the gospel. And Communism as a government, that's OK, but as a religion, that doesn't really satisfy a soul. And it really cannot make Really Living. Only by accepting Jesus, which can really comfort our hearts and provide living water for our souls. That is proved by the search of the nation, of my family, and of my mother. And me as individual. Only accepting Jesus, we are Really Living!"

Rebekah's mother's search, then, stands as an example to China and to all of the world. Her mother is well educated. She is well versed in Taoism, Buddhism, Confucianism, Communism, and many other philosophies.

But her heart was never touched, never warmed, never watered with the love of God, until she met Jesus. That's when she began Really Living.

# With God in the Valley

## Sandy Wyman Johnson

How do you walk through the rough places in life, the valley of the shadow of death, where the fear of evil besets you, even though you know that God is still with you?

My interview with Sandy Wyman Johnson began on a cheerful, upbeat note as we talked about the joys of motherhood. But I knew we were headed for rough country, where we would talk about the bumps and tragedies that life throws our way. Still, I wanted to hear Sandy's story, and even more than that, I wanted her to tell me what she had learned as she walked through one of the most difficult experiences a parent can ever face.

Sandy is what I would call a natural-born mother. She loves everything that has anything to do with babies and children. She told me that even as a little girl, people knew she would make a good mother someday. "I brought home baby everything," she said. "Everyone knew I couldn't wait to have children. I was babysitting the neighborhood children, and at church, I loved to be with the babies. There was just a real call— always I knew in my heart I couldn't wait to be a mom."

When I asked Sandy how many children she had, she said without missing a beat, "Well, I count Trevor still, so three."

The words *I count Trevor still* carried a lot of weight, but she said them cheerfully.

We talked a lot about Trevor—what a loving, caring, cheerful boy he was. He had red hair, dancing green eyes, and freckles set on a sturdy body.

"Trevor relished everything in life; he tasted everything in life," Sandy told me. "He could tell you how the bird was feeling when it was singing. He was our little resident artist; he loved to color, and from the time he was little, he would include great detail.

"Kids fought over who was going to sit next to him on the school bus. Babysitters would ask permission to take care of Trevor the following week. There was just something very endearing about him. He was mischievous, but he was thoughtful and kind. He was the only child I ever met who made out his Christmas list of what he wanted to give to other people before he made out his list of what he wanted to get. He started doing that when he was about four."

Things went along just fine for Trevor until just after Christmas when he was six years old. The first sign of trouble came when the school principal called Sandy and told her that Trevor was starting to experience motion sickness on the school bus every day.

Well, of course, that can happen to anyone, so it wasn't a matter of great concern.

Then about three weeks later, Sandy and Trevor were in the car together, when Trevor said, "Mommy, I see two trees, I see two of you, and two cars." That was a little worrisome, but soon it cleared up, and even though Trevor was dizzy from time to time, it seemed like maybe just one of those things that happen to children as they grow.

By the time March rolled around, though, other symptoms started to appear. One day when Trevor was playing with a group of kids, running up and down a hill, he came into the house looking pale and said he felt funny.

Sandy took him to the pediatrician that very afternoon, and after examining him, the doctor sent them to have Trevor's eyes checked. The optometrist sent him to a pediatric ophthalmologist, who pointed out that Trevor had a condition called *nystagmus* that causes the eyes to jump about when a person looks to the side. The ophthalmologist recommended a magnetic resonance imaging (MRI) scan, and when the results of that test came back negative—showing no detectable problems—it was cause for great rejoicing.

Sandy said something very interesting when she told me about this: "I remember thinking at that time, how interesting it is when I jump around and dance for joy, and I'm so pleased when things go the way I want them to, and I say, *Thank God!*

"Would I be able to say that—is God still just as merciful—if I had gotten a different result?

"But I quickly shooed that from my mind because I didn't have to think about it, because Trevor was going to be fine."

You have to know the rest of the story to understand just how profound those thoughts coming from Sandy were.

Despite the encouraging results from the MRI scan, things continued to go downhill for Trevor. Sandy began to notice that her normally irrepressible little boy didn't have his usual spunk. He wanted to lie down a lot. His speech also sounded a bit nasal. Then she saw a slight tremor in his left hand. "Over the ensuing weeks, it was like watching him have a slowly evolving stroke," she said. "Very subtle, but every morning there would be something new or more pronounced."

The next stop on what would become a long, tortuous circuit of medical visits was to a neurologist's office. There, a second MRI scan turned up no particular reason for concern. Maybe it was just a virus, the doctor suggested. But by the end of March, Trevor was in such distress that he could no longer go to school. He had to stay in bed all day, lying on his right side to keep from becoming dizzy and nauseated.

A pediatric neurologist suggested that maybe Trevor had picked up a case of encephalitis, and that given a few weeks, he would feel much better. Soon though, the little boy had to be hospitalized. Steroids, physical therapy, occupational therapy—nothing seemed to help. He couldn't even sit on the edge of his bed for more than a few seconds without becoming dizzy.

After two weeks in the hospital, Trevor went home, where he continued to receive physical therapy and occupational therapy. But by this time, he could barely sit up, and it was hard for him to even swallow. "After three weeks at home, he said, 'Mommy, I'm not getting any better. I think you need to call the doctor.'"

Sandy called the pediatric neurologist, who said that if his previous diagnosis of encephalitis had been correct, Trevor should have been better by now. He needed to see Trevor again, which of course meant another trip to the hospital and another MRI.

On the way to the waiting room after the scan was complete, Sandy happened to glance into a room where four radiologists were studying images on film. Ominously, all four of them were shaking their heads and looking very concerned.

"For the first time, I allowed myself to admit what we might be dealing with," Sandy said.

It seemed like an eternity before the pediatric neurologist

came to the waiting room. He was a kindhearted man who loved children, and he had a little boy just about Trevor's age.

And as soon as she saw him, Sandy could tell that he had been crying.

The doctor sat down with her and made sure she was firmly planted in her chair before he spoke. "I wish I didn't have to tell you what I have to tell you," he said. "But it appears that Trevor has a very fast growing cancer in his brain stem. He probably has only a few weeks to live."

How does a mother cope with that sort of announcement?

"Don, I remember feeling like—and I'm sure others know what this is—like all the air had been sucked out of the room," Sandy said with tears in her eyes. "I wondered when I would be able to take my next breath."

How can you handle news like that about a sweet, kind, innocent, loving little child? How do you fit something like that into a world where a loving God is in charge?

I think Sandy's response was pretty standard for a person who has grown up claiming the promises of God and seeing answers to prayer. "I began trying to claim Scripture, trying to come up with a formula that would make God do what I wanted Him to do!" she said. "Your life really does flash before you, because it's not something you have control over. You can't fix it. There is a great need to surrender.

"But you don't know that yet."

What Sandy did know was that the next thing she needed to do was to talk with Trevor and tell him what was going on. But how would he respond?

Trevor had celebrated his seventh birthday just three weeks earlier. When Sandy shared what the doctor had told her, "He held my hand and began to cry," she said. "And then he said, 'Mommy, at least I had seven years. Some people don't even have that.' "

*At least I had seven years!* Can you imagine a little boy who so loved life, who just a few weeks earlier had been full of life and mischief, taking that kind of news with such courage?

I've had a lot more than seven years of life, and I don't think I could handle news like that so calmly.

"Over the next two weeks, he became our little teacher," Sandy told me.

Two weeks. That's all the time they had with him.

His condition worsened rapidly. Radiation treatments that were supposed to make him more comfortable ended up making things worse, so they were discontinued.

Then, during the second week, Trevor developed a kidney stone that caused him great pain.

Sandy confessed that this turn of events made her really angry at God. Why this on top of everything else?

But then Trevor's doctor came to her and told her that because of the stone, he was recommending that they increase his pain medication. "We can medicate him to a place of comfort. In which case it'll just take a few days, but he can sleep," the doctor said.

Could this be a blessing in disguise?

How do you accept a blessing that means that the child you love so much is going to go to sleep, and he won't wake up until he hears Jesus call his name on resurrection morning?

Sandy was very honest with me about how she reacted. "I had to have a couple of hours to go into a separate room. I literally lay on the floor and screamed and kicked, and felt very naked and vulnerable before God. I remember lying, just stretched out arms and legs, and just saying, 'Take me instead'—you know. 'Take me!' " Her voice began to break here, and she paused before continuing. "But I felt a peace begin to come."

Having worked through her anguish and accepting the peace that God was giving her, she put on her mommy face again and went to see her little boy. "I went in to Trevor, and I said, 'Trevi, the doctors can't believe how brave you've been. You've been a spiritual giant for all of us.' I told him the doctors said they had some medicine that they could give him for this severe pain, 'And you will be able to just be comfortable and go to sleep.'

"When I said 'sleep,' his eyes got real big, and I knew he knew what I meant, and he squeezed my hand, OK."

Trevor went to sleep then, and two days later, he took the last breath that his little lungs will draw until the day that Jesus comes again.

## Walking with others through the valley of shadows

How can a mother go through an experience like that, a dark valley where prayers seem to go unanswered, with her faith intact? Is it possible to come out the other side still believing in a loving God? Might it even be possible that going through such a rough place could be turned into a platform or stepping-stone to help a person be a greater help to others walking through the valley of shadows?

In Sandy's case, the answer is Yes!

She has spent much of her life in hospitals working as a nurse. But since Trevor's death, she's had a change of professions. Now she's a hospital chaplain. She spends many days walking beside others who are facing their own times of darkness, weeping with them, and just being there for them as they ask hard questions about life.

She doesn't always have adequate answers, but at least she understands the questions.

"Why?" is a question she often hears people asking. It's one I know I've struggled with as well, when trying to help someone cope with a tragic situation.

Sandy shared a fascinating perspective on that question. " 'Why,' I've learned, is not really a request for information; it's just a searching for deeper meaning and purpose." She went on to explain that to her, the deepest cause of suffering for many people is not the pain they are going through, but rather the sense of futility that develops if they can't see any purpose in it. Helping a person see that there is a God who cares and who walks with us through the valley, can do a lot to alleviate suffering.

But just sharing that information is not what people need most, as she explained later. What they usually need most is another human being to walk beside them in their difficult time.

Another question chaplains and other ministers often have to face is, Where is God when it hurts? Drawing on her own experience, Sandy says, "I've learned that He's really in me, the one who is hurting. He's not in the thing that hurt me. I am all through trying to explain God and what He is up to. What I've learned is, I'm a creature, and He is the Creator, and someday, when I'm face-to-face with Him, I have no doubt that He will make it plain. It probably will be something that I would have chosen had I really understood all the picture and understood what was happening."

Sandy has also wrestled with questions about whether God causes things like this to happen, or just stands back and lets them happen. And she's come to the conclusion that that's not really the question she needs to answer. "If He caused it to happen, if He allowed it to happen, it doesn't matter to me. Because I am still choosing whether to let Him be God. Why would I want the God of the universe to withhold from me any experience that would deepen my walk in the world, my sense of gratitude, my sense of compassion for other people, my capacity to have a big heart and show up in other people's lives and try to make some sense out of the world that's so hurting?"

For me, that brought up another question that I had a feeling Sandy would have some good answers to, so I asked her for advice. What can we do, how can we best be of help to someone who is walking through the valley of the shadow of death?

She had a ready answer—several answers, in fact. "What helped me most was people who came alongside and didn't try to fix my sadness, didn't have an answer to take me out of it, didn't try to make me feel better. You don't need to feel better, you need to experience what you're experiencing. We all need this struggle, so that we can get to the deeper places within us."

So, just being there for people, not trying to answer their questions, not trying to cheer them up or help them look on the bright side, is the key. Sandy put it this way: "People don't need explanations when they're hurting; they need consolation. They need to know that somebody cares about how they're doing, that they're not going to be abandoned. Some of the best comfort that I had was silence; it can be the best gift of all. Or somebody just said, 'Sandy, I don't know how you're getting through this, it doesn't seem fair to me either. It's tragic.' And then weep with me. Just be in those moments."

That was powerful advice—advice that some of us might find difficult to follow, especially if we're inclined to try to find an answer or explanation for everything that happens. Sandy had a special caution for people who want to share a biblical answer with a person who really just needs someone to sit quietly beside them. "Even people who are religious will often show up at a tragic event in somebody's life and begin giving Scripture and so forth. And, my how wonderful that is at the right time—but there are times when that is not what's most comforting. Human beings are God's language, and so I think God heals us, and we are healed through being present for each other."

We can find healing by being present for each other in the hard places of life. What a precious perspective that is! That's what Sandy is doing now, and that's what she encourages all of us to do, if we want to be Really Living!

# A Life Given to Those in Need

## Terri Saelee

Terri West (now Mrs. Terri Saelee), a Nebraska girl, was living a fairly uneventful life in the heart of America when she received a phone call that would change her life—and not only hers, but the lives of thousands of people who needed to know Jesus as their Savior. Thousands of people who had little hope and needed someone to come and help them learn how to start Really Living.

Terri was finishing her freshman year at Union College in Lincoln, Nebraska, when her phone rang one day. On the other end of the line was the vice president of the college, Dr. John Wagner. "Would you mind coming to my office?" he asked. "There's something I'd like to discuss with you."

Uh-oh. I don't know how that would make you feel, but having been a bit of a mischief maker all of my life, I'm afraid I would have been sweating bullets, as they say, all the way to the administration building. What rumors about my little pranks had reached the presidential suite? Was this the end of my college career? Would I even get credits for all the course work I'd done so far this quarter?

But I doubt that Terri was as nervous as I would have been.

Knowing her as I do, I doubt that she had been involved in any questionable campus capers.

Turns out she didn't have had much to worry about. "Are you familiar with the refugee situation in Southeast Asia?" Dr. Wagner asked when she was seated across the desk from him.

Terri had to admit

that she'd heard about refugees, but that she didn't know much about their situation. This was in 1982, when tens of thousands of people whose lives had been disrupted by the Vietnam War and the spillover turmoil in Cambodia and Laos were still living in refugee camps in Thailand.

Many of these people had no hope of ever being able to return home. Their families had been killed, they had ended up on the losing side in the war, or they had been displaced by the brutal Pol Pot regime in Cambodia. They no longer had a home in their native land, and they would probably be imprisoned or killed if they tried to return.

"These people live in primitive huts in camps populated with tens of thousands of refugees," Dr. Wagner explained. "Our church, working with the Adventist Development and Relief Agency [ADRA] and several independent organizations, is sending volunteers to assist in meeting the daily needs of these people."

Terri is a naturally softhearted woman. As images of thousands of suffering children and adults played across her mind's screen, she heard Dr. Wagner asking a question. "Would you be willing to consider going as a student missionary to help out in the refugee camps?"

Would she? Well, it would mean missing a year of school, she supposed.

"As you probably know, most student missionary assignments are for a full year," Dr. Wagner continued. "But because the situation in these camps is very tenuous—you never know from one week to the next how long a camp will be open; the Thai government has a way of keeping things off balance—this assignment would be for only six months."

Just six months. She could certainly share that much of her life with people in desperate need. And besides, it sounded like an adventure. She loved listening to the reports of student missionaries who had come back from distant lands. Now she could have her own exciting stories to tell!

A few weeks later, Terri, accompanied by Dr. Wagner's wife, Lilya, and several other student missionaries, flew to Bangkok, Thailand, and went from there to the Ubon refugee camp situated near the border with Cambodia.

I asked Terri what life is like for people living in a refugee camp. The camps where she worked were administered by the United Nations Border Relief Operation (UNBRO). All that the residents could do was sit and wait for other people to make decisions about their fate. Would they be sent to live in Australia or perhaps in Canada or the United States? Or would their plea for asylum in a third country be denied, and would they be forced to return to hostile conditions in their home country?

But the people weren't content to just sit and wait. Most of them were very industrious, raising herb gardens, growing fruit to sell, weaving baskets, finding whatever way they could to make a little extra money to cover their expenses.

"Even the little children had to work hard," Terri told me. "One morning I saw a little five-year-old girl who was carrying water in two buckets on a stick across her shoulders, up a rugged hill—actually the steep side of a mountain—to her little hut. I thought, *Wow if she can do it, I should be able to.* So I tried. I couldn't get it up the hill without help! I got halfway up, spilling along the way, doing my very best. And I grew up on a farm! I got only halfway up, and somebody had to relieve me. But this little girl got all the way up that hill with her water. It's incredible!"

Terri went on to tell me more about living conditions. "The places they sleep were hard. They don't have beds, so they split bamboo into strips and nail it to other pieces of bamboo, and if they can afford a mat, they put a mat and maybe a little blanket on it."

For the first several months that she was there, Terri taught English and other classes to the refugees. She wasn't sure she should try to convert them to Christianity. After all, they had their own culture and religion.

But then one day, her attitude made a 180-shift.

"It was a terribly dark day," she remembers. "I had been teaching there five months. I went to the camp one day, and it was just—just terrible sadness. I said, 'What's wrong?' and they said, 'Did you hear? They made an announcement this morning.'

"The reason I was there teaching them English was that these people had been told they would be able to resettle in another country. But they had just been told, 'Oh, I'm sorry. There's been a mistake.'"

The mistake meant that thousands of people who had been promised an opportunity to resettle in a country where their lives wouldn't be threatened were now being told that their only option was to return to the country they had fled.

In the meantime, they would be sent back to a camp farther north on the Laotian border. But the worst part of the news was that aid workers like Terri would not be allowed to go there because the people in that camp were going to be repatriated, and they didn't need to learn English.

Seeing the sadness and despair on her students' faces, Terri was brought up short. "It brought me back to my real reason for going. God loves us! And He wants us to share His love with others.

"So what had I been doing teaching just English for five months and not even mentioning the name of Jesus? All of a sudden there was no point in me teaching English, and so I sang them a song in Thai.

"On the road of life
There's no hope to be found,
Not a shadow of the things that we hoped for.
But on the road of God there is hope
There's hope to be found.

"I had just learned this song. It was a beautiful song written by one of the teachers at the language school. And when I sang this song for my students, they said, 'Why didn't you sing this song before? Why didn't you tell us about Jesus before?'

"By now I had only perhaps a week with them before they would be shipped off to another camp that they said I could never go to. So all of a sudden—forget English! Let's teach them what really matters, because I realized they might never come to my country, but if they get to know Jesus, then they can be ready when Jesus takes us all to heaven, and we won't have to deal with all these issues.

"So, I was able to buy little copies of the books of Matthew,

Mark, Luke, John, and Acts, and I gave them each a copy. Then I realized—when they go, they won't even be able to write to me—they don't have money to buy stationery. So I bought some stationery and some pens and pencils and sent them with them."

Soon the refugees were sent north to Ban Napho. The student missionaries had been told they would never be able to go to that camp. "But," Terri said—a determined look on her face—"we prayed.

"It was a four-hour trip. So, we prayed, and we decided we're going to try it!

"When we arrived there, we gave the Thai guards a list of our students. They said they couldn't call all those people, but they did call the first few on the list and let us just inside the gate to talk to them. They gave us twenty minutes, and we talked to them. It was wonderful. We told them, 'Keep learning about God. He's preparing a better place—even if you can never go to America, heaven's a lot better than America, let's meet there. We don't know if we'll ever see you again here, but let's meet there. Learn all you can. Get to know Jesus, and He'll take you home with Him when He comes.' "

The next time Terri and the others went, the guards gave them an hour with their students. Then the next time they were preparing to go, one of the missionaries said, "You know, I think God will help us to be able to go to their homes this time. Let's pray!" And pray they did—prayer meetings every day. And the prayers were answered. They were allowed to visit in the people's homes, which was a real thrill and a real blessing, both for the missionaries and for the refugees.

"It was in that camp," Terri told me, "that a young man told me his story. He was in his midteens at the time, and he told me that he and his family had lived in Vientiane, the capital of Laos.

His parents were well-to-do physicians, but when Communism came in, they were taken to a reeducation camp."

The young man and his sister were left to fend for themselves. They tried everything they could think of—even raising fish in their bathtub. But to no avail. Finally, they had to flee to a refugee camp.

"As he was telling me this," Terri said, "he said he had never seen his parents again. He didn't know if his parents were dead or alive; he didn't know if he would ever see them again. But then he said, 'But I am glad that Communism took over my country.' My mouth dropped open, and I said, 'Why?' And he said, 'Because if the Communist soldiers had not taken over our country, I would never have learned about God.'

"It means that much to these people to know about God," Terri told me excitedly. "You know, I think that sometimes those of us who grew up knowing about Jesus just take it for granted, and we don't realize what a tremendous hope God has given us."

Seeing that kind of joy among the people she was teaching, Terri was hooked. She'd committed to just six months of mission service, but she kept extending her stay—it was four more years before she finally returned home. Sometimes she even worked in camps where there was no stipend available to pay her—she had to ask friends and family back home to help. Other times she was able to find work in schools that could pay her a small amount to teach English.

Finally, she decided it was time to return to her home country and complete her own education. Can you imagine what a culture shock she experienced when she arrived back in the United States?

The first time someone took Terri to a restaurant in San Francisco, she could barely stand to eat. Ten dollars for a bowl of soup? It seemed inconceivable to her. With each bite she could see the faces of children in refugee camps—children whose fathers have become opium addicts because of war wounds and the hopelessness of their situation. She could see the children's faces—tears running down through caked dust—standing by the market, looking at the food. "They would not beg," Terri says. "But they would stand and look at the market, and look at the people buying things; and if you would buy them something, for two Thai baht, which is eight cents, you could buy them a full meal. That's if you bought them a bag of noodles, which would be a meal for them. Or, if you had the kind of lunch I had every day—sticky rice and fresh papaya salad—that was four baht."

Seeing those faces in her mind's eye, Terri had a hard time enjoying her lunch.

Her love and concern for the people of Southeast Asia stayed with her when she enrolled in a Christian college not far from Sacramento, California.

As she looked around the campus, she began to feel something like she had experienced in the restaurant. She was among people who had had plenty of food—spiritual food—all their lives. "I felt, what am I doing here? Everybody here already knows God. What is my life worth here? And I asked God that, and His answer was, 'Terri, just let Me love you.' "

She felt God's love there, and she felt that her own spiritual batteries were being recharged. Then at a Week of Prayer meeting, a speaker said something about how all Asia had heard the gospel during the ministry of the apostle Paul. And suddenly a new thought came to her. A lot of people from Asia were living in the Sacramento area. Could she use the languages and intercultural ministry skills she'd learned in Thailand to reach out to them?

And so it was that even in the United States, Terri found a mission field. "I did a little research and found out that there were five thousand Hmong refugees living in Sacramento!" she told me. She used that information as the basis of an informative talk she had to give in speech class. But she wasn't content to just share information.

"The next assignment for speech class was a persuasive speech."

What do you suppose she persuaded the students to do?

You guessed it. "My topic was 'Weimar College should have an outreach to the Southeast Asians in Sacramento.'"

Terri is a pretty persuasive lady. By the next quarter, the college had established just such a program. "And guess how many students signed up?" she challenged me.

"You," I said.

"Yes. And twelve more—just the number of disciples!"

Soon Terri and the students began taking surveys among the people she wanted to reach. One of the first people she met spoke all of the languages she had been learning, and he took her to meet the leaders of the various ethnic groups in his apartment building. The students inquired whether any of the people could use help learning English or anything else. Of course a lot of people could. With one day's contacts, they found plenty of work to do for the entire quarter.

The story goes on from there—Terri soon found herself serving as a part-time employee of the court system because she volunteered to serve as an interpreter for a refugee who had gotten in trouble with the law. After she served as his interpreter in court, she was surprised to receive a check in the mail a few days later, paying her for her service to the court.

It turns out that the court needed interpreters, and they were all too happy to hire her pretty regularly. Now she was able to use the languages she had learned while serving as a student missionary to earn money to help pay her college expenses.

But, of course, she didn't just serve as an interpreter for the people she met. Long before in Thailand, she had learned that just meeting language needs wasn't enough. These people needed to know their Savior as well, and by God's grace, doors began to swing open, allowing Terri to share the gospel.

One day she volunteered to help a family whose father and husband had been thrown in jail because someone had accused him of doing something he hadn't done. She wasn't able to get the man out of jail, but in the process of trying to help, she learned that the rest of the family needed help with their applications for permanent residency.

At seven o'clock one morning, Terri went with the family to submit the forms, but found that even that early in the morning they were at the end of a long line. After waiting all day, they were nearly to the front of the line when Terri saw another family attempt to submit forms. "I could tell that none of them spoke English, and the person behind the desk looked at their form and said, 'This is wrong! This is wrong! This is wrong! Go back, and fill them out and bring them back another day.' "

Terri's heart went out to these people—she'd had her own experiences with trying to meet government requirements in a country where she didn't speak the language. "I thought, *Another day of this?* So I went up to them, and I said, 'Would you like me to help you?' And they said, 'Oh, could you?'

"So I went to their home, and on the way out, the lady said, 'Do you go to church?' and I said, 'Yes.' 'Can I go to your church?' "

Of course Terri's answer was Yes. "And they just thrived on learning about Jesus," she told me.

While working with the Southeast Asian people in Sacramento, Terri found that there were churches where some of the Adventists who had come from that part of the world would attend, but that the other people in the church didn't even know who they were or where they were from.

One church in particular had Karen people attending, but the other members hadn't gotten acquainted with them. (The Karen [pronounced *ka-REN*] are a tribal group from Myanmar, among which there are many Adventists who have suffered heavy persecution under the military regime there.) The Karen would just come to church and slip out before the members got a chance to visit with them. She helped the Karen refugees set up their own worship, and soon there were eighty people attending!

Terri's heart is very much invested in the people of Southeast Asia—and refugees from all around the world. Today, she's married to a Hmong gentleman she met at Southern College (now Southern Adventist University), and they live in Wisconsin, where her husband supervises work in congregations of Southeast Asians in two states. For her part, Terri remains active in helping refugees from all over the world. She serves as the refugee ministry coordinator for the North American Division of Seventh-day Adventists.

Terri told me that there are about fourteen million refugees scattered around the world, so I asked her, "What should Christians be doing for these people?"

"I love a quote I read somewhere," she said. " 'It is acquaintance that awakens sympathy, and sympathy is the spring of effective ministry.'

"You know, I could give you methods," she continued. "But the best thing, I've discovered is to get acquainted with some refugees—sometimes just driving around town, just finding someone that you can tell doesn't speak English fluently—or contact refugee agencies, or just look in the restaurant portion of the phone book and see what cultures are here once they've been established.

"But new refugees often are clustered in little pocket communities, and we're not aware of them. They're afraid to venture out, because they don't know the language. But if we find out about them and go to them, I haven't found a single one that wasn't overjoyed.

"In American culture, we're not supposed to go visiting if we're not invited, but in most other cultures, if you don't visit, it means you don't care."

Talking to Terri, you can't help but be moved by the plight of the refugees. And you can't help but be moved by the depth of caring she shows. I know she inspired me with a new resolve to reach out to people around me. I hope reading about her has inspired you to do the same.

Because when we reach out and touch others with the love of Jesus, that's Really Living!

# Using God's Gifts for His Glory

## Virginia-Gene Rittenhouse

Virginia-Gene Rittenhouse threw away her future at the age of seventeen, but quickly got it back again, courtesy of her Father in heaven. And since then she's helped hundreds of other seventeen-year-olds (and younger and older kids too) learn to trust in God and experience the rewards of living by faith.

I really enjoy meeting and talking with people to whom God has given a special gift. To meet people with two special gifts is even better. And I would put Virginia-Gene in that category. She is amazingly gifted in the area of music, but God has also given her the gift of an amazing faith.

The gift for music began to manifest itself very early in her life. She told me that she began composing—both words and music—when she was just three years old. At that time her parents were missionaries in South Africa, and even though her mother was a music teacher, they couldn't afford a piano.

When Virginia-Gene was six years old, the family moved to the campus of Helderburg College not far from Cape Town. The thing that Virginia-Gene remembers best about

149

that move is that soon after they moved, they found a secondhand piano to buy.

"As the men tried to move it into the house, I was trying to play something on this piano, right while they were moving it. Mother said, 'Wait! We have to get it moved!' I was so excited that I couldn't even wait till they got it moved inside."

When the piano was finally situated, Virginia-Gene's mother sat down with her for a few minutes, pointed out where middle C was, gave her a book, and showed her the treble clef and the bass clef; then she left Virginia-Gene on her own. "By nighttime I could play the entire book through. I gave myself the first lesson, and that evening, I played Mother the concert."

Virginia-Gene isn't one to brag, mind you. As we talked, she was constantly giving glory to God for the way that He has blessed her with talents and success.

A few years later, when Virginia-Gene was ten years old, her parents brought her to the United States when they came home on furlough, and someone in Portland, Oregon, heard about this young prodigy and invited her to play some of her own piano compositions on a local radio station. That's right, at the age of ten she played her own compositions on a live broadcast!

When the family returned to South Africa, Virginia-Gene's reputation preceded her, and soon she had a request from the South African Broadcasting Corporation to perform. She loves to tell a funny story about how, when she was rehearsing, a well-known violinist from London heard her and remarked that there was nothing so special about her—that people shouldn't get so excited and spoil her. "She's not much of a composer," he said. "But I will give her this; she did play Bach quite well."

It turned out that the joke was on him. He was the only one who thought she was playing Bach. Everyone else knew she had been playing her own composition. The poor man became the laughingstock of the country because he couldn't tell the difference between a Bach piece and the composition of a ten-year-old.

Virginia-Gene's performance for the broadcasting group won her a scholarship to study violin, piano, and composition at the University of Cape Town. She was able to study there for the next seven years.

By the time she was thirteen, she had been invited to play with the Cape Town Symphony. The first time the orchestra members heard her play her violin, the reaction she heard was, "That little girl must love God; otherwise she could never play Bach the way she did!"

That was just one of the many times when Virginia-Gene would have the opportunity to give glory to God for the gift He had given her. People were so impressed with her playing that she soon became a regular part of the symphony, performing many concerts with them over the next four years.

Then came the day when she made the decision to throw away her future. At least that's what her professor told her she was doing. But to Virginia-Gene it was more like casting her bread, by faith, upon the waters (see Ecclesiastes 11:1).

She was just seventeen years old when she was selected as

one of ten contestants to be sent to Pretoria, the executive capital of South Africa, to compete for the London Associated Board Overseas Scholarship—the most prestigious music award anyone in South Africa could win. The prize would be a scholarship to study at the Royal Academy in England.

"I'll see you on the train to Pretoria Saturday morning," her professor told her on Friday afternoon. The audition was to be held on Sunday, and the professor wanted all of his students to arrive a day early so they would be well rested when their time to perform came.

"Oh no," she told him. "I won't be taking the train on Saturday morning; that's my Sabbath. I'll take the train Saturday night."

"No! You need to be on the express train Saturday morning. The Saturday night train is slow. You won't get to Pretoria until two hours before you're scheduled to perform. You have to be on the morning train!"

"I'm sorry. I can't do that."

When the professor saw how determined she was, he just threw up his hands and sent her away. "You're giving up your whole future just because of that Sabbath! That's ridiculous! Get out of my sight!"

It was a real trial of faith, I'm sure. I'm also sure that, looking back on it, Virginia-Gene is happy that she stood the test. There would be many more times during her life when she would face similar trials, and when she did, she could always look back to that time when God honored her decision to stand up to her professor.

And so after taking the night train to Pretoria, Virginia-Gene arrived at the concert hall just an hour before she was to perform. She heard later that the judges had been so impressed by one of the students who had performed in the morning that they didn't even want to come back to hear the students who were scheduled for the afternoon. They already knew whom they were going to give the award to.

But then they heard Virginia-Gene, and their opinions changed. She was awarded first prize, along with the scholarship to study at the Royal Academy. Because her parents were scheduled for furlough back in the United States that year, she requested permission to use the scholarship at the Juilliard School in New York, and permission was granted.

Virginia-Gene's music education continued at Juilliard, and later at the University of Washington, Boston University, and the Peabody Institute Conservatory, where she earned a doctorate in piano and violin.

In the 1940s, '50s, and '60s, she taught music at Walla Walla College and Atlantic Union College, and for a brief time in Jamaica. But her main claim to fame is, of course, the New England Youth Ensemble, which came into being almost by accident.

It happened in 1969, when Virginia-Gene was teaching music to several young people in her home. "I started with four young kids in my living room," she told me. "They were little students of mine, and I thought if I got them to play together, maybe they'd like to practice more."

"You were playing a trick on them!" I said, accusing her good-naturedly.

"I tricked them!" she confessed with a smile.

After they had been practicing together for a while, she got them an appointment to play at a local church. "My idea was just to take them to one or two churches and help them practice a little. I had no idea I was founding an orchestra." Then the local Kiwanis club invited them to play at its Christmas dinner. "After we performed, these men's responses were unbelievable. Some of them had tears in their eyes. They said, 'You have restored our faith in American youth! This was the most remarkable thing. They played Bach and Handel, and they're just kids!' "

At that point the woman who had a gift for music and the gift of faith began to believe that God had something bigger in store for her little crew of musicians. And she was eager to find out what that was!

By the time of the General Conference Session in Atlantic City, New Jersey, in the summer of 1970, Virginia-Gene had a bit larger orchestra practicing together, and they were invited to play at the session. "People just went crazy over this young orchestra!" she told me.

Since that time, the New England Youth Ensemble has performed in forty-five different countries, played for heads of state, and had a positive influence on the lives of hundreds of young people.

Virginia-Gene just bubbles over with stories about her experiences in taking the young musicians to various parts of the world, and she especially likes to talk about the times that their faith was tried and then God answered their prayers.

There was her first trip to China, for instance, traveling with both an orchestra and a choir. Government officials gave them very strict instructions: there was to be not one sacred word in their concert. They agreed to this because they were planning to perform secular classical music. But there was one little oversight. Nobody remembered that the coronation anthem they planned to perform ended with the words *Hallelujah, Amen.*

Those words might have slipped right past the Communist officials except for one thing. A group of Christians had sneaked into the concert uninvited, and when they heard those words, they went wild. They said it was the first time they had heard those words sung in twenty-five years.

The crowd was calling for an encore, but the officials stormed onto the stage and forced the orchestra and choir to leave the stage and locked them up in a room, forbidding them to speak to anyone. Things kept going from bad to worse as officials came and went, threatening to cancel the entire tour and burn the brochures they had printed.

The musicians were finally sent back to their hotel, and there they stayed for three days, waiting to see what would come of this, continually praying for God to intervene and let them continue their trip through China. Government officials on both sides of the ocean became involved, and messages were flying back and forth between Beijing and Washington, D.C.

When the dust finally settled, it was decided that they would be allowed to continue their tour. "We went all over China— oh, my word! At the end of the tour, we played in Beijing on national television to an audience, we were told, of probably a million listeners! And the Chinese government said, 'Any time you can return to China, you may play at any place. Everything will be open to you!' It was a miracle, just a miracle!"

Through the years, the group has made four trips to Poland. The second one was their most memorable. They were supposed to play at six o'clock in the evening for a mass at a major cathedral in Warsaw, but the truck that was supposed to transport them to the cathedral didn't show up at their hotel until 6:00 P.M. It was pouring down rain, and by the time they got to the cathedral, the mass had already begun, and the priest wasn't at all happy to see them come traipsing soggily in with their equipment in the midst of his service.

By coincidence, President Gerald Ford was in town that day, on his way to the Conference on Security and Cooperation in Europe being held in Helsinki, Finland. The American ambassador's wife had been so impressed with the Youth Ensemble that she had invited the president's social secretary to come to the church to hear them perform. But with all the delay and confusion, the secretary grew weary and decided to leave early.

That was a tremendous disappointment to Virginia-Gene and the ensemble because the ambassador's wife had suggested that they might be invited to perform for the president. "I went to the altar. I remember I was in the cathedral, and I prayed that the Lord would work some miracle. Well, He did. At eleven o'clock that night, we got word: bring down all the forms and the passports of all your kids. The next day, they said, 'Just be ready at a moment's notice.' And at twelve o'clock, they said, 'We're taking you to the Wilanów Palace, where the president is staying.'

"We got to the palace, and they said, 'We won't allow anyone in the palace. The president is here, and it's too risky. We can't allow a whole bunch of kids to come in.'"

But the ambassador's wife was insistent, she went in and begged for permission to bring the ensemble in, and finally permission was granted for them to go in and rehearse. The social secretary attended that rehearsal and was so impressed with what she heard that the group was invited to play at the reception for President Ford that night.

When the reception was over and everyone had left, the group was taking down their equipment, getting ready to load up and leave, when they heard tapping at the door. Virginia-Gene's husband went to see what was going on, and who should he meet but President Ford himself, all alone!

The president had been so impressed by the group that he

said he had escaped from his security detail and had come back on his own, just to spend some time with the kids. He spent about twenty minutes with them, visiting and telling them how proud he was of them. Later, in Helsinki, he mentioned the group in a speech, saying how proud they made him of American young people.

Virginia-Gene shared more stories about performances in other countries, as well. She's so excited about the way the Lord has used her and the musicians she has been privileged to work with. She told me of young people whose lives have been completely transformed by their experience in playing with this Christian group. She also told me about a trip to Russia during which the Communist officials admitted to being envious of what this group had—they thought these kids would make great Communists, ideal Communists, but confessed that they had no way to motivate their young people to that kind of excellence.

Since 1982 the ensemble has had a special relationship with the famous English composer and conductor John Rutter. The way this came about is another testimonial to the influence of faith in God in the group's history. The ensemble had already done two benefit concerts at Carnegie Hall in New York City when they were selected by MidAmerica Productions to be the orchestra that would participate in a special event during which Rutter would conduct choirs from all over the United States.

This was a tremendous honor, and things were going along fine until Virginia-Gene was told that the rehearsal was to begin at ten o'clock on Saturday morning. "No!" she said. "We are a Seventh-day Adventist group, and we won't be rehearsing on Saturday morning." The manager from MidAmerica tried to persuade her that this was an opportunity that she really shouldn't pass up, but she was adamant. Her group would not be rehearsing secular music on the Sabbath.

"Then you'll have to explain that to John Rutter," the manager said.

He picked up the phone and dialed Rutter's number, then handed the phone to Virginia-Gene, and she proceeded to explain the Sabbath to him. There was a long silence when she finished, and then finally Rutter asked, "What time is your sunset?"

"It's 4:16 on Saturday."

"All right. The rehearsal will begin at 4:17."

And that was the end of the conversation.

So, at 4:17 P.M. the orchestra was in its place. Rutter stood up, looked at his watch, and said "It's 4:17." Then without further ado, he picked up his baton and began to conduct a difficult Bach piece.

"And he didn't stop!" Virginia-Gene told me. With other orchestras he often stopped constantly to correct their performance, but the New England Youth Ensemble went straight through the piece without a hitch.

MidAmerica Productions reported to Virginia-Gene the following day that when Rutter had gone out to dinner with some of their staff, all he could talk about was how well the ensemble had played.

That began the close relationship that continues today. Rutter has conducted the group many times since, and twice when the group has been passing through England on tour, he has invited everyone to his home for a meal. "He talks about our religion. He says to me, 'If I had young people who are deeply religious like yours are, what I would do!' " Virginia-Gene told me. But in her heart she knows it is not *religion* that makes her kids the great musicians they are—that *faith* has a lot to do with it. "We have our Friday evening prayer fellowship, and there is where we pray for our work. I tell them, this is the most powerful moment in all of our rehearsals. The most important is our prayer fellowship, because it's that which has given us these great experiences. I want them to understand that we should be grateful for what God has done through music and through their talents. It has changed their lives—many of their lives—completely!"

Virginia-Gene Rittenhouse is Really Living! And because of her influence, countless young people and audiences all over the world have had an opportunity to witness what Really Living by faith is all about.

# REALLY LIVING